STATE V. BAKER

Case File
Trial Materials

Fourth Edition

Katherine E. Donoghue
Stetson University
College of Law

Joseph E. Taylor
University of the Pacific
McGeorge School of Law

NITA®
NATIONAL INSTITUTE FOR TRIAL ADVOCACY

Address inquiries to:

Reprint Permission
National Institute for Trial Advocacy
325 W. South Boulder Rd., Ste. 1
Louisville, CO 80027–1130
Phone: (800) 225-6482
Email: permissions@nita.org

ISBN 979-8-88669-006-4
FBA 2006
eISBN 979-8-88669-007-1
eFBA 2007

Printed in the United States of America

ASPEN
PUBLISHING

Official co-publisher of NITA.
aspenpublishing.com/NITA

SUSTAINABLE FORESTRY INITIATIVE Certified Sourcing
www.forests.org
SFI-00756

Contents

Acknowledgments

- Dr. Heidi Sievers, PhD, MSFS, CBPA, CCSI, for providing high-velocity gunshot blood spatter photos (Exhibit 22).
- Elizabeth Boals, Associate Professor of Law and Director of the Center for Excellence in Advocacy at Stetson University College of Law, for her mentorship.
- Joseph E. Taylor, his colleagues at University of the Pacific McGeorge School of Law, and the various law enforcement agencies who helped create the early editions of this case file.
- Bryan Duggan, for everything.

INTRODUCTION

This is a criminal case in which Sarah Baker, the daughter of a billionaire international arms dealer, has been charged with the first-degree murder of her husband, Kelly Baker, a well-known Nita City television news anchor. On September 7, YR-1, Sarah Baker shot her husband, Kelly Baker, in the kitchen of their large estate known as Ashgate Farm near Warrenton, Nita. Kelly Baker was found lying face down on the floor. A 9mm Luger pistol was found on the floor near his body, and a butcher knife was in his right hand. Four bullet wounds were found in his chest and neck area.

In her statement to the police, Sarah Baker said her husband had accused her of having an affair with Kendall Johnson, the chief deputy district attorney of Darrow County. She denied the relationship, explaining that she had worked with Johnson to establish a new center for battered women through a nonprofit organization she chaired. She said that on the morning of September 7 she was in the kitchen sometime after 8:00 a.m. when her husband entered the kitchen, brandished a semiautomatic pistol, and said that he was going to kill her for being unfaithful. She was able to convince him to put the gun down. Sarah Baker then said that she grabbed the gun to protect herself, and as soon as she did, Kelly grabbed a butcher knife, screamed obscenities, and advanced toward her, threatening to kill her. She said he slashed her left arm with the knife. As he came after her, she fired to protect herself, shooting him four times. A defense forensic pathologist has concluded that the autopsy findings are completely consistent with Sarah Baker's version of events.

The State contends that Sarah Baker intended to divorce Kelly and to cut him out of her will, but that Kelly told her he would sue her for a large portion of her estate because they did not have a prenuptial agreement. For that reason, the State claims, Sarah Baker decided to kill Kelly and claim self-defense by slashing her own left arm, planting the knife in his hand, and staging other evidence in the house. An autopsy examination showed that Kelly Baker suffered fatal wounds to the neck and thorax (chest) as well as wounds to his right arm and back. Three shots hit him at downward angles. The State's forensic pathologist concluded that the gunshots were consistent with Kelly Baker being seated when he was shot and further concluded that the four knife wounds on Sarah Baker's left arm were superficial and consistent with wounds that had been self-inflicted. A State's firearm examiner concluded that the absence of gunpowder residue on Kelly Baker's clothing meant that Sarah Baker was more than four feet from Kelly when she fired.

The applicable law is contained in the jury instructions set forth at the end of the file.

Electronic copies of all exhibits are available at

http://bit.ly/1P20Jea, password Baker4.

Special Instructions

When this case file is used for a full trial, each party is limited to calling the following witnesses:

State of Nita:
Detective Casey Lee
Dr. Morgan Kahn
Forensic Scientist Dannie Rodriguez
Kit Manville

Defendant:
Sarah Baker
Dr. Leslie Torres
Kendall Johnson
Chris Spanalski

Discovery Obligations

Pursuant to Nita C.C. § 1054.2, all police, investigative, forensic, scientific, and medical reports, documents, records, statements, recordings, diagrams, and photographs were disclosed to the defense by the prosecution.

Pursuant to Nita C.C. § 1054.3, the defense has disclosed to the prosecution all names, addresses, statements, and reports of the witnesses the defense intends to call at trial.

Required Stipulations

1) The Federal Rules of Evidence and the Federal Rules of Criminal Procedure govern this case.
2) All witnesses may be played by any gender. However, it is stipulated that the defendant Sarah Baker is female regardless of whether the person playing such witness is male or female. No argument may be made that the physical description of the person playing the witness does not match a description provided in the case packet. For ease of use, this case file utilizes the singular "they" when discussing all characters except the Bakers.
3) The parties stipulate to proper chain of custody for all evidence seized in this case.
4) The parties stipulate that all exhibits are accurate and authentic—that is, that they are what they purport to be. However, this stipulation does not prohibit either party from objecting to the admissibility of certain exhibits based on the Federal Rules of Evidence (subject to the stipulations contained herein) or arguing to the jurors in summation that such evidence may not be reliable given the facts presented at trial.

5) Dr. Kahn and Dr. Torres have reviewed all materials contained in the case file.

6) The search warrant inventories and returns, as well as the subpoena and responding affidavit, are true, accurate, and complete copies of the originals filed with the court by Detective Lee.

7) Exhibit 1, the transcript of the 911 call, and Exhibit 2, the recording of the 911 call, are both accurate and complete.

8) The "Last Will and Testament of Sarah Baker" is a true, accurate, and complete copy of the only will prepared by the defendant.

9) The report of Senior Identification Technician Robin Mulligan (Exhibit 21) is admissible in its entirety by either party at any time without objection. No Confrontation Clause objection, or any other objection, may be made to the admission of Exhibit 21. The parties also stipulate to Mulligan's qualifications to render the opinions set forth in Mulligan's report. This stipulation, however, does not prohibit counsel from seeking to admit other evidence regarding Mulligan's credibility.

10) The Amazing Alex recording (Exhibit 20) is admissible in its entirety by either party at any time without objection.

11) The affidavit of Amazing custodian of electronic records (Exhibit 19) is admissible in its entirety by either party at any time without objection. No Confrontation Clause objection, or any other objection, may be made to the admission of Exhibit 19.

12) The pictures contained in composite Exhibit 22 (22-A and 22-B) are of the same wall. The color difference is the result of varying light exposure from the camera.

13) The transcript of each witness's testimony has been excerpted so that only the witness's answers are reprinted. The testimony presented is a true and accurate rendering of that witness's answers.

14) All years in these materials are stated in the following form:

    - YR-0 indicates the actual year in which the case is being tried (i.e., the present year);
    - YR-1 indicates the next preceding year (please use the actual year);
    - YR-2 indicates the second preceding year (please use the actual year);
    - etc.

15) The applicable law is contained in the jury instructions set forth at the end of the case file. The jury instructions as written may not be changed, but counsel may ask the court to give additional instructions to the jury based on the evidence presented at trial.

Pretrial Motions

1) The defendant moved to suppress all statements she made to Detective Lee on Fifth, Sixth, and Fourteenth Amendment grounds. The court ruled that the statement given at 1010 hours was admissible, but the defendant's comments at 1700 hours exercising her right not to talk were inadmissible.
2) The defendant moved to suppress all evidence seized, and any testimony related thereto, on Fourth and Fourteenth Amendment grounds. The court denied the defendant's motion to suppress.
3) All Confrontation Clause objections were litigated pretrial and overruled.
4) These legal issues may not be reraised or relitigated at trial.

Criminal Indictment

IN THE DISTRICT COURT
OF THE STATE OF NITA
COUNTY OF DARROW

THE STATE OF NITA	)	
	)	
vs.	)	
	)	Case No. CR-2201-23
SARAH H. BAKER,	)	
Defendant	)	
	)	

THE STATE OF NITA does hereby charge the defendant, SARAH HANNA BAKER, with the following offense under the Criminal Code of the State of Nita:

That on 7th day of September, YR-1, at and within the County of Darrow and within the boundaries of Nita City, SARAH HANNA BAKER committed the crime of Murder in the First Degree in that she, with premeditation and the intent to cause the death of Kelly Baker, caused the death of Kelly Baker, a human being, in violation of Section 101 of the Criminal Code of the State of Nita.

DATED: October 25, YR-1

Lonnie Voiselle

Ella Marie Wright, Attorney General

By Lonnie Voiselle, Deputy Attorney General

State of Nita

Exhibit 1

Transcript of 911 Call

The following is a transcript of the call received by Dispatcher Edel Karl of the Darrow County Sheriff's Department from Sarah Baker at 8:51 a.m. on September 7, YR-1:

Karl: 911, what's your emergency?

Baker: Ah, yes. I need . . . I need to report a . . . shot man and he's dead.

Karl: Where at?

Baker: He's at Ashgate Farm and. . . .

Karl: What's the address?

Baker: 8714 Springs Road. Ashgate Farm.

Karl: OK, what's his name?

Baker: Ah . . . Kelly Baker. He's my husband.

Karl: OK, did you just find him or . . . .

Baker: He tried to kill me.

Karl: OK, did you shoot him?

Baker: I . . . I had a gun, yes.

Karl: Did you shoot him?

Baker: I think he's dead.

Karl: OK. Is anybody else in the house with you or anything?

Baker: Nobody at this time.

Karl: Can you tell me ah . . . have you had problems before?

Baker: Yes, I have.

Karl: OK. Where's the, ah, weapon at, ma'am?

Baker: It's . . . it's on the floor in the kitchen.

Karl: OK. I just want to make sure you don't have it when the deputy shows up, 'cause you might be a little antsy when the deputy gets there, so you just want to make sure that you don't have it.

Baker: No, it's . . . it's on . . . it's on the floor.

Baker: Chris . . . Chris, please come here. Don't go in the kitchen. Kelly is dead. . . .

Karl: Right. . . .

Baker: . . . I'm on the phone. Please, Chris. . . .

Karl:	Right, make sure nobody goes into the kitchen.
Baker:	The sheriffs are coming right away, Chris. Sit down. Sit down.
Karl:	Make sure nobody goes in there.
Baker:	No. Nobody, nobody . . . .
Karl:	OK, ma'am, I need you to come out the front door . . . .
Baker:	OK.
Karl:	. . . and meet with the deputy.
Baker:	OK, I will.
Karl:	OK.
Baker:	I will hang up now.
Karl:	OK, that's fine.

Exhibit 2

Recording of 911 Call, 8:51 a.m. on September 7, YR-1

(Call available at http://bit.ly/1P20Jea, password Baker4)

Exhibit 3

KNIFE FOUND IN KELLY BAKER'S RIGHT HAND

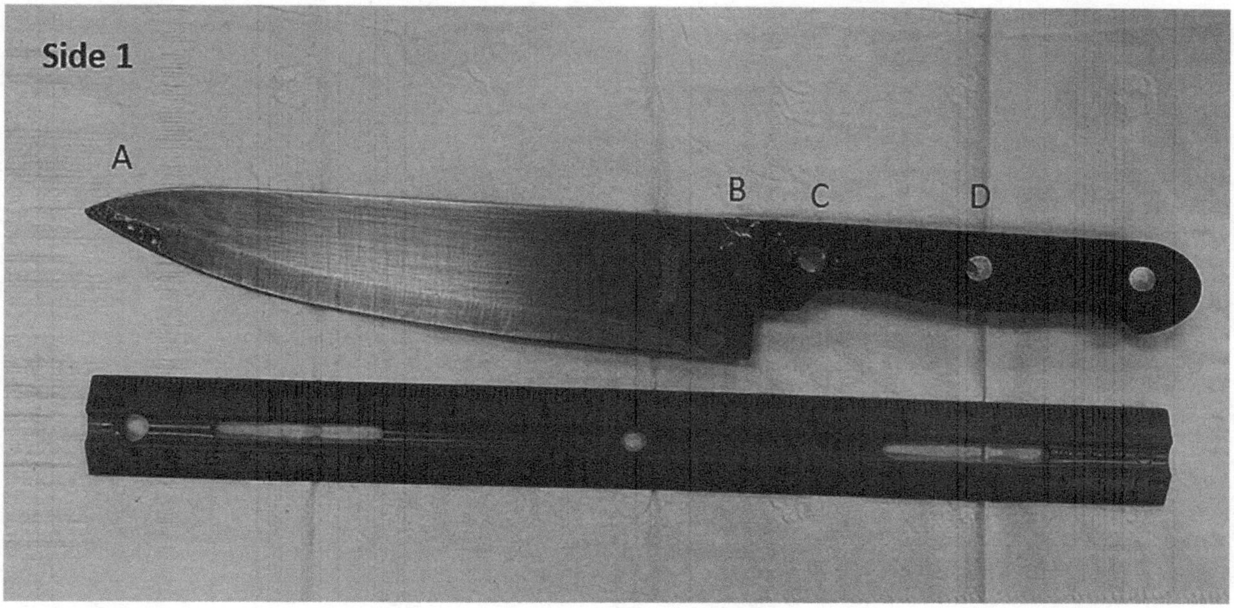

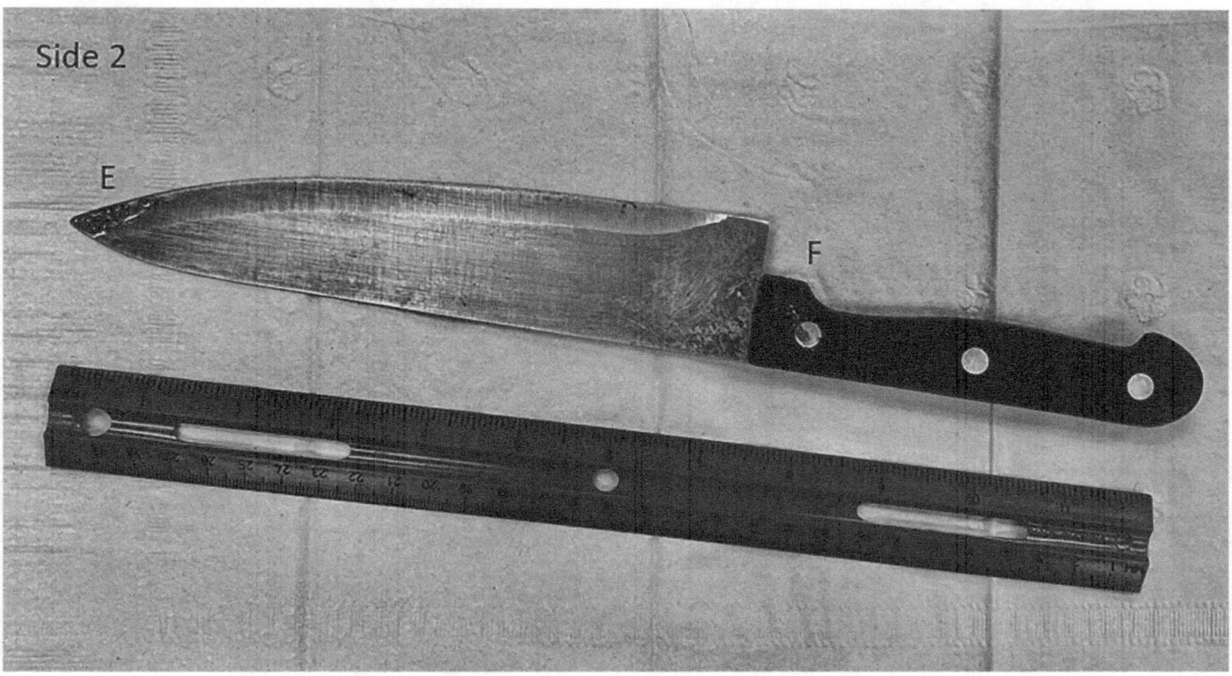

Exhibit 4

9MM LUGER PISTOL AND MAGAZINE

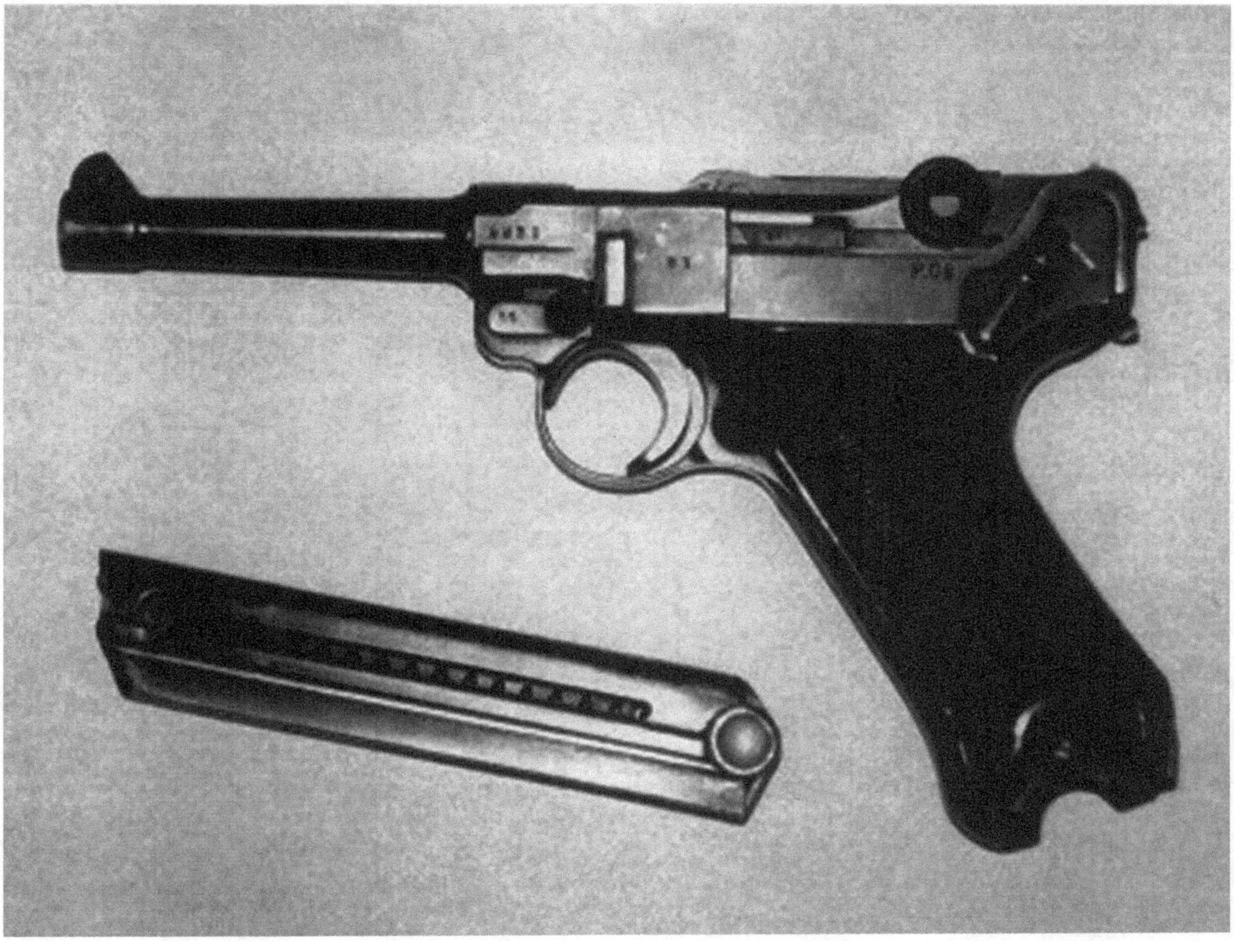

Exhibit 4

9mm Luger Pistol and Magazine

Exhibit 5

Ashgate Farm Main House

Exhibit 6

Diagram of the Kitchen Crime Scene

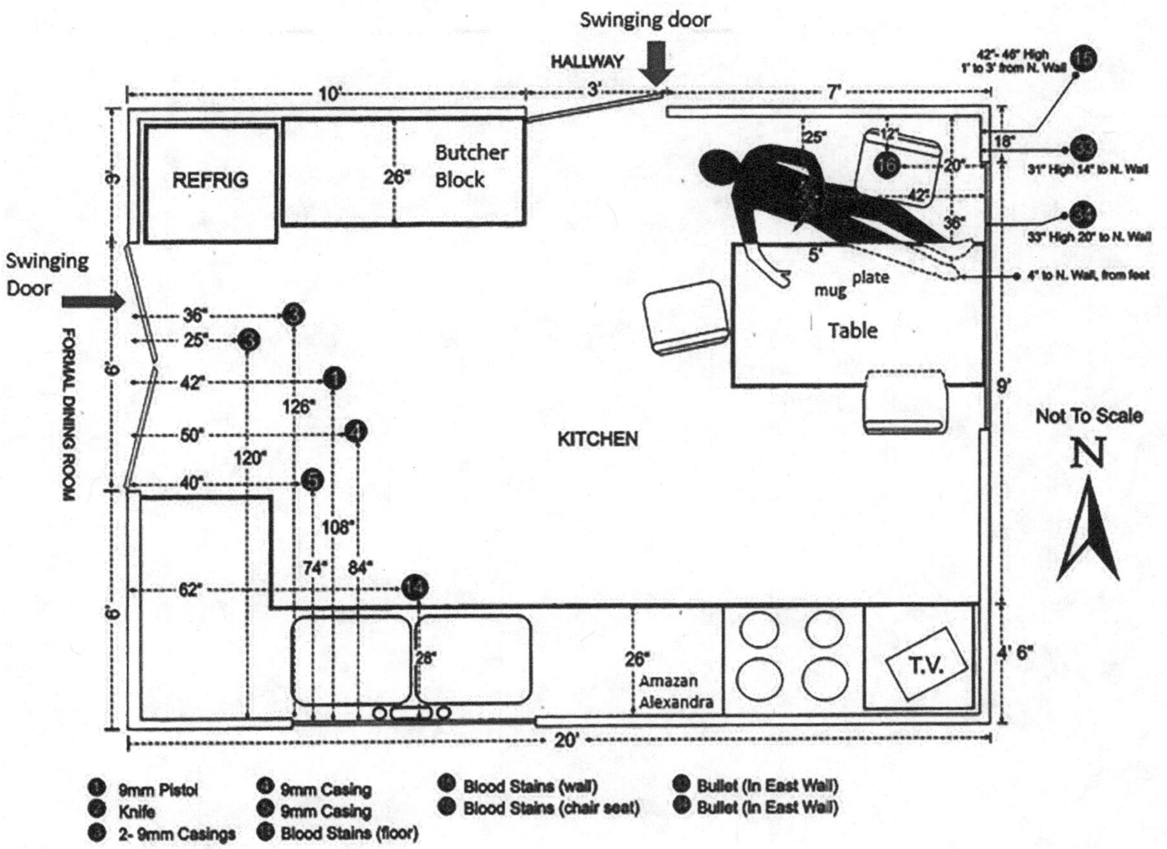

Exhibit 7

Kitchen Elevation Sketches

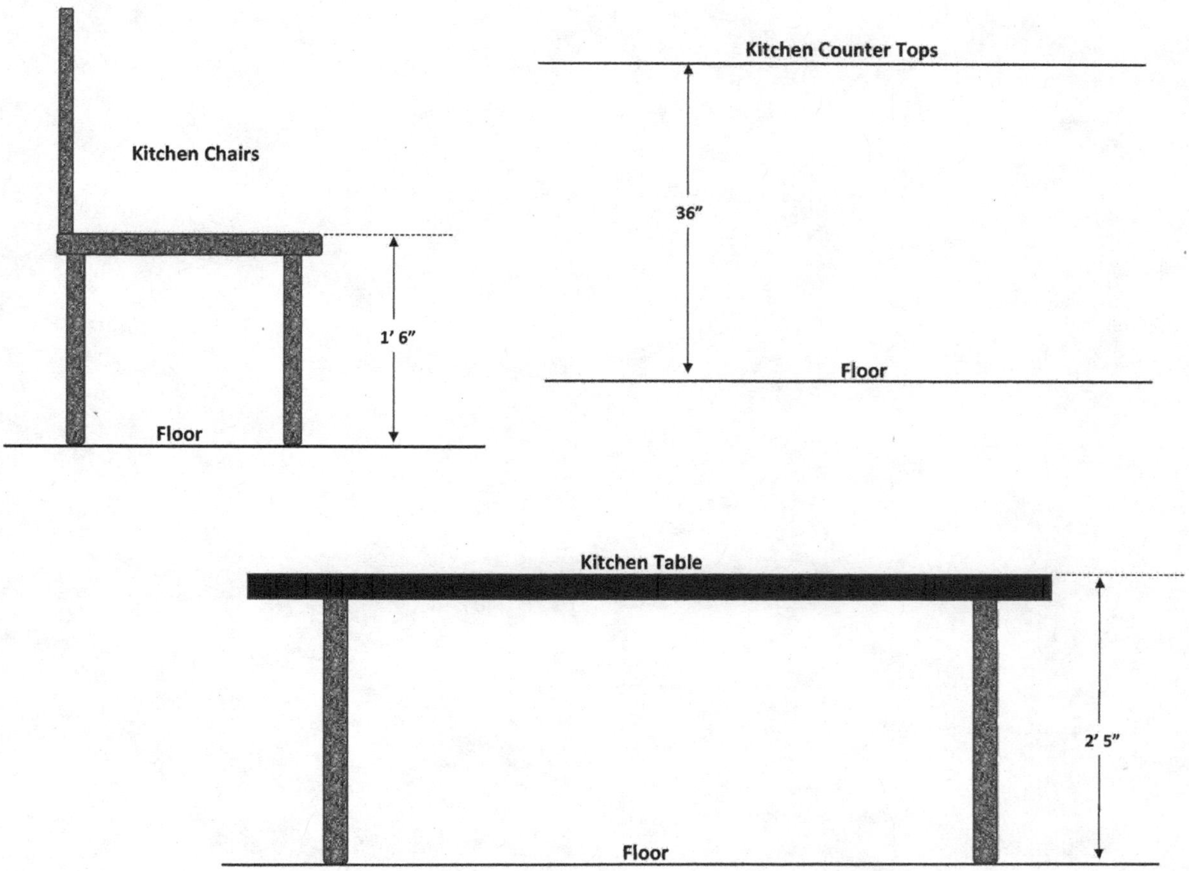

Exhibit 8

Diagram of Ashgate Home

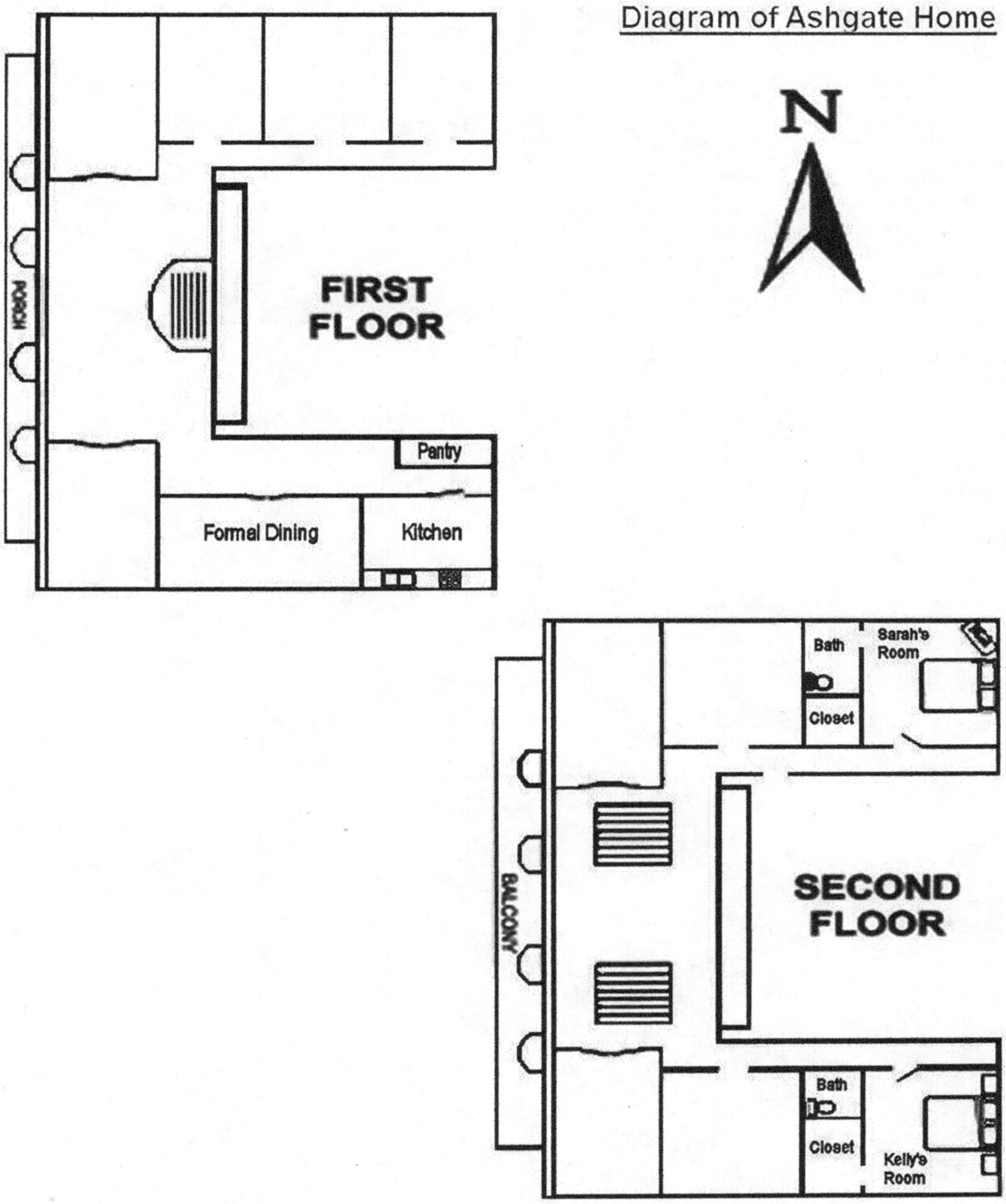

Exhibit 8

Diagram of Ashgate Home

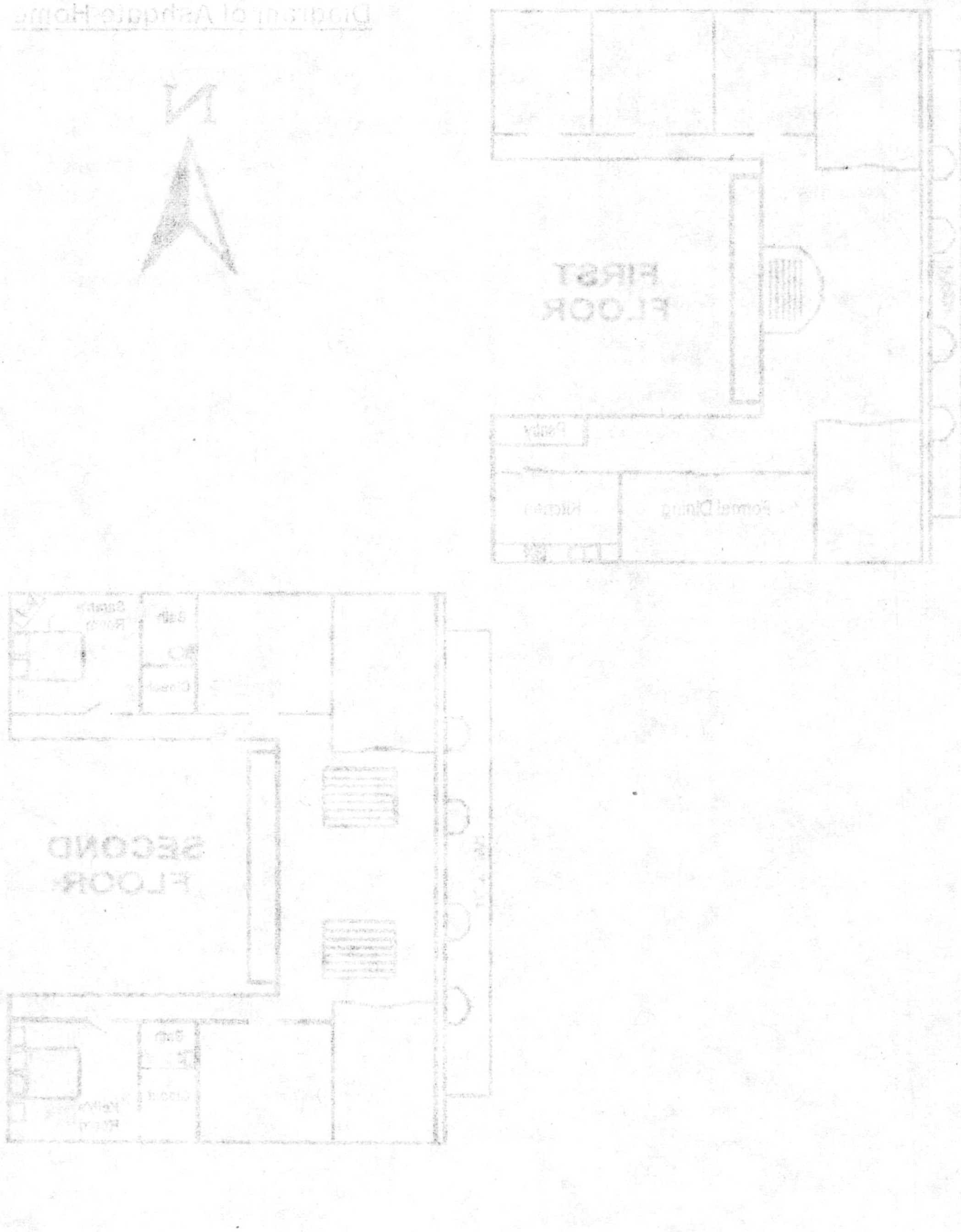

Exhibit 9

DIAGRAM OF ASHGATE FARM

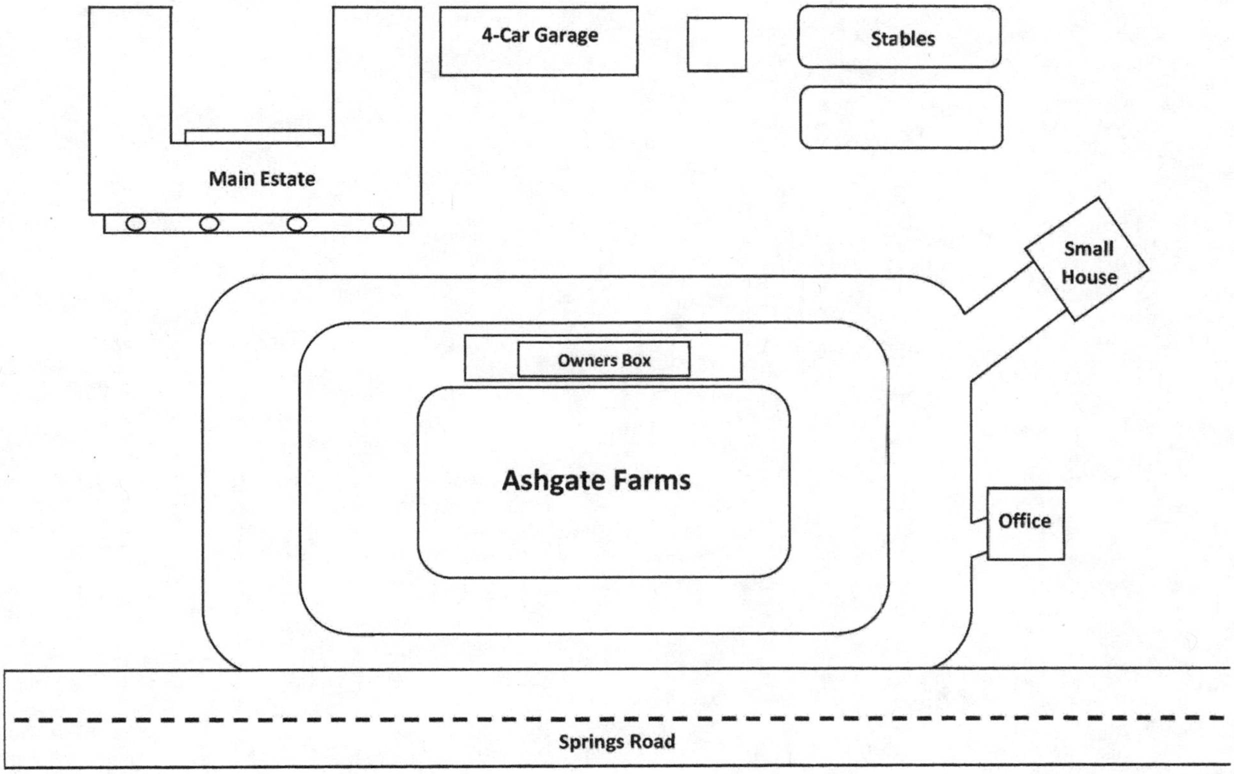

Darrow County Sheriff's Department
Nita City, Nita
Offense Report #YR-1–28088
Report entered: 09/7/YR-1

Incident Type/Offense	Location	Reporting Officer
CC 100—Homicide	Ashgate Farm 8714 Springs Road Warrenton, Nita	Detective Casey Lee Badge Number 114
Date/Time Reported	**Date/Time Occurred**	
9/7/YR-1, 08:51		

Persons		
Role	**Name**	
Victim	Kelly Lawrence Baker	
Arrestee/Suspect	Sarah Hanna Baker	

DCSD Offense Report
CC 100—Homicide

Initial Investigation

At 0852 hours I received a radio call from Dispatcher Edel Karl to respond immediately to a homicide scene at Ashgate Farm near Warrenton. I communicated via radio with Deputy Camelli, who informed me that they were en route and would control the scene and contact the Coroner's Office. I arrived at 0910 hours. The Ashgate estate is approximately 350 acres and includes a large, U-shaped, two-story home and several outbuildings, including a four-car garage and several stables. Deputy Camelli was standing with two people she introduced as Sarah Baker (female, age 40, 5'9", weighing approximately 150 pounds) and Chris Spanalski. Deputy Camelli said they met Sarah Baker and Chris Spanalski upon arrival at 0857 hours. Ms. Baker was standing outside the home at the front entrance door when Deputy Camelli arrived. Deputy Camelli then entered the home and was unable to locate any other people present in the house. They saw the body of Kelly Baker, Ms. Baker's husband, lying face down on the kitchen floor. Deputy Camelli checked and found no vital signs. Deputy Camelli then waited outside with Ms. Baker and Chris Spanalski for my arrival.

I went to the kitchen of the Baker home. I saw Mr. Baker's body, which was lying face down in front of the chair that was facing the TV/closest to the hallway entrance (see Exhibit 6). I also saw a breakfast plate and coffee mug sat on the table in front of the chair that faced the TV; a 9mm Luger (serial # 6851) and four shell casings in the area of the refrigerator; and two bullet holes in the wall near Mr. Baker's body. There was blood on the floor and what appeared to be a kitchen knife in Mr. Baker's right hand, which was partially under his body. I also saw a kitchen towel near the sink that appeared to have some blood on it. Not wanting to leave weapons unsecured at the scene, I put on gloves, collected the pistol, which had three live rounds in the magazine and one in the chamber, the shell casings, and the knife and placed them in evidence bags. The Luger pistol is a semi-automatic, which I know from my training and experience means the gun automatically ejects shell casings every time a bullet is fired. I then walked outside and secured the bags in my police vehicle; at this time I retrieved evidence placards and went back into the kitchen and marked where I had located each item for later forensic investigation.

The deputy coroner, Clem Beazley, and the county forensic pathologist, Dr. Morgan Kahn, arrived shortly thereafter. They entered the kitchen and examined the body. Dr. Kahn stated that the body was not yet in rigor mortis (stiffening of the body approximately two hours after death), indicating that the victim had died within the last two hours. Dr. Kahn drew a chalk outline on the ground indicating the body location and positioning, took custody of Kelly Baker's body, and left.

I saw that Ms. Baker had scratches and bright red blood on her left arm. Ms. Baker requested permission to change her shoes in an upstairs bedroom. I told her to take her shoes off now, placed them in an evidence bag, and then walked with her upstairs where she put on a new pair of shoes. I then communicated with Dispatcher Karl, who informed me of the contents of the 911 call they had received from Ms. Baker, including that she sounded very calm.

Based on my examination of the scene and my understanding of the 911 conversation between Dispatcher Karl and Ms. Baker, I arrested Ms. Baker for homicide and transported her to the Darrow County Jail, where she was booked and printed. At the jail and in my presence, Ms. Baker was examined by county nurse Alex Kouri. Ms. Baker's left arm was washed, and the nurse stated that the cuts did not appear life-threatening and did not require sutures or bandaging. With Ms. Baker's consent, Nurse Kouri took samples of hair and a blood sample from Ms. Baker. Nurse Kouri removed Ms. Baker's clothes from the dressing room and handed them to me for safekeeping as evidence. I took custody of one pair of women's pants and a short-sleeved blouse. Ms. Baker was issued a standard prisoner uniform.

At 1010 hours I fully informed Ms. Baker of her *Miranda* rights. Ms. Baker told me that she understood those rights and was willing to waive them and tell me what happened. See suspect's interview and statement beginning on the following page of my report.

Statement of Sarah Baker

Ms. Baker said the events that morning were the culmination of several weeks of disagreements between her and her husband. She said it was important I understand the background of their marriage. She is 40 years old, and Kelly is 42 years old. They met four years ago. At the time she was a successful breeder of polo ponies, and she was an avid polo fan. At her Ashgate estate every July she held an annual charity polo event known as the "Community Games." She said the proceeds of the event are distributed to local charities. Kelly Baker was covering the event for a local news station, and he interviewed her. The two began to see each other more, and one year later they were married. The two lived at her estate, and Kelly drove to Nita City from Warrenton almost every day for work. Because of Kelly's schedule, they didn't see each other much.

In August YR-2, Ms. Baker felt it was necessary she become more involved with the community rather than just spending all her time working out and riding horses, so she accepted an offer to become the unpaid director of Project WEB (Women Experiencing Battery), a nonprofit organization devoted to protecting abused women. She realized she was in a position, because of her wealth and influence, to acquire more funding for the organization. In early YR-1 the Board of Directors authorized her to develop a new Center for Battered Women where victims could reside safely away from their abusers and obtain mental health treatment and other support services. She began meeting with community leaders to coordinate the development and planning efforts. During this process, she met Kendall Johnson, the deputy chief district attorney of Darrow County. Johnson introduced her to others in the county government, and the Darrow County Battered Women Council was formed. Ms. Baker and Johnson co-chaired the council, and as a consequence they met on a regular basis to plan or implement the effort. Ms. Baker said that while she greatly admires Johnson, she has no romantic feelings for Johnson.

In July YR-1, Sarah once again hosted the Community Games at her estate. However, this year a good deal of the charity income was earmarked for the WEB Center. Kendall Johnson attended and sat in the owner's box with Ms. Baker. Mr. Baker was not present, as he had other work. After the event, Ms. Baker and Johnson conferred about the proceeds, and they had a "working dinner" at a nearby restaurant. There were others at the restaurant who knew Mr. Baker, and apparently someone mentioned this to him. That night he became especially irate and called her a lot of bad names. She was surprised because she had never seen this side of her husband before. Ms. Baker denied any illicit behavior, but Mr. Baker became very angry and verbally abusive: he said he didn't believe her lies, that she "belonged to him," and that she needed to treat him "with the respect he deserves." She said he yelled, "If I find out you're sleeping with Johnson, you'll be lucky if you get the chance to move into your new fancy facility."

Ms. Baker thought that if she kept her distance from her husband he would eventually cool down and see that there was nothing going on between her and Johnson. For the last several weeks, she tried to avoid Mr. Baker. The two exchanged a few text messages, but otherwise she did not see him much because the cook prepared their meals and they had separate bedrooms. She said the only contact she had with him was when she would occasionally see him at breakfast. He liked to get up early and have breakfast in his pajamas, whereas she liked to sleep in and would never be seen without being fully dressed and ready for the day. So, she would only see him in the kitchen briefly as she was heading in to get breakfast and he was finishing up.

About a week ago, Mr. Baker called her on his way home from work and told her he expected her to be there when he got home. He arrived at about 8:00 p.m., and he appeared to have been drinking. He was unsteady on his feet, yelling, and slurring his words. He screamed that she was making a fool of him, and he had heard that she had been "sleeping with Johnson in our home." She told her husband that Johnson had been there several times for planning sessions for the center and that there was nothing romantic between them. Kelly reached over and picked up a China lamp that was a family heirloom and said, "This is what I want to do to you," and threw the lamp against the fireplace, shattering it into pieces. Ms. Baker cried and ran from the house, got in her car, and drove to the home of Chris Spanalski, the manager of Ashgate Farm, where she stayed the night.

Ms. Baker said she began to fear that her husband would hurt or kill her. She thought about the will she had prepared shortly after her marriage, leaving virtually her entire estate to Mr. Baker. She decided to contact her lawyer and revise the will to cut Mr. Baker out with the exception of a summer house and a car. She said nothing for several days, but on September 6th, Mr. Baker again called her on his way home from work and told her to be home when he got there. Ms. Baker and Chris Spanalski were finishing a discussion on the front porch when Mr. Baker arrived. He had again been drinking, and without waiting for Spanalski to leave, he snarled, "So you're going to cut me out of the will, are you?" She begged him to be quiet, but he repeated the same statement. She said Spanalski then left, and she and her husband walked into the house. Mr. Baker said, "I know what you're going to do. You're going to dump me for your fancy DA. If you so much as give cutting me out another thought, I'll make sure you never live to do it." She said Mr. Baker then put his fingers in the shape of a gun and pointed them at her and said, "I mean it. I loaded that Luger a while back and I've never been afraid to use a gun."

Ms. Baker said she wanted to leave the house again, but decided that this would just anger her husband more, so she quietly went to her bedroom. She said she was terrified, locked her bedroom door, kept her loaded revolver under the pillow, didn't sleep most of the night, and got up very early the next day. She said she was constantly worried he would use the pistol she knew was in his room. She said both of the guns were hers, registered to her, and were given to her by her father, Elton Martin, who owns an international arms-dealing corporation. She said that she kept the revolver in her room and that Mr. Baker had the semi-automatic pistol in his room, which was the gun he threatened her with the next morning.

The next day was the cook's day off. Ms. Baker said around 7:30 a.m. she went to the kitchen where she fixed a croissant and coffee. She sat in the chair on the far side of the table facing the TV and watched the morning news. Around 8:00 a.m. she got up from the table to wash her hands. She was standing at the sink when her husband came in through the swinging door to the hallway. She turned around and saw him walk in. He looked like he had been up all night drinking—he was disheveled, slurring his words, and unsteady on his feet. He called her an "unfaithful bitch" and she again told him he was being "crazy." He then pulled the Luger out of his robe and pointed it at her. She said that she realized she had to do something quickly and had to get control of the gun. She told her husband to look through the text messages on her cell phone that was on the kitchen table—passcode 110088—so that he could see for himself that there was nothing going on between her and Johnson. He put the gun on the corner of the table closest to her, turned his back, picked up her cell phone, and began to look through it. As his back was turned, she quietly inched toward him and was able to grab the gun off the table while he was distracted by her phone. But he noticed as soon as she grabbed the gun. He called her a "stupid bitch" and said she "would pay" as she was backing up toward the formal dining room. Mr. Baker then grabbed a large knife from the butcher block on the counter next to the refrigerator and lunged toward her, waving the knife back and forth. She was trying to get the gun safety unlatched, but her hands were shaking. They struggled, during which he cut her left arm a few times with the knife, but he was so unsteady on his feet that she was able to push him away from her and he stumbled backward toward the table. He then called her a bitch again and lunged at her with the knife and she fired the gun until he dropped. She said her husband dropped to the floor and made a few gurgling sounds and then was quiet. She could see blood all over the floor and on her arm and shoes. She didn't know what to do but ran to the sink area to grab a dish towel to stop the bleeding on her arm.

She then retrieved her cell phone from the ground and called Chris Spanalski and asked Chris to come over immediately. She said Chris arrived about five minutes later, and Ms. Baker showed Chris what had happened. Chris then said that they had to call for help, and told her to call 911. Ms. Baker then called 911 and explained what happened, and the 911 operator told her not to touch anything, leave the gun in the house, get out of the house, and wait for the sheriffs to arrive. She and Chris did that.

I asked Ms. Baker whether she had ever fired guns before. She said that obviously she had some experience with guns, because her father was a major gun dealer, and she owned two guns. I asked if she had ever had to use one before. She said other than attending firearm safety training and periodic target training, the only incident was about one and a half years ago when she had to use one for protection on her property. She said that an irate former customer had come onto the grounds of Ashgate Farm around 7:30 in the evening and was yelling in front of her home. She went out and asked what was wrong, and the man said he had been cheated, that his pony had died, and called her a fraud. He said he wanted satisfaction right then. Ms. Baker said that she was frightened, as the man appeared to be headed for her front porch. She said that the only employee on the property was an incompetent drunk who was useless, so she ran inside, got the gun, and fired off several rounds in the air and told the man to leave. She said it worked, and the man ran down the road to his car and sped off. She said later she was issued a citation for unlawfully firing a weapon within an incorporated area. After conferring with her attorney, she decided to plead no contest and paid a fine. I asked Ms. Baker who the incompetent employee was, and she said, "Kit."

I informed Ms. Baker that our department would continue our investigation and asked if she would give us consent to search her cell phone, which was already in our custody along with her clothes, as well as reenter her home for the purpose of conducting additional investigation, including searching and seizing relevant evidence and conducting a forensics investigation. She said, "You've already arrested me for a murder I didn't commit, so no, you can't go back inside to plant evidence that will support your theory of what happened." I told her she had the right to refuse, and we would simply apply for a search warrant instead.

I typed up the section of my report titled "Statement of Sarah Baker" and gave it to Ms. Baker to review, make any necessary corrections or additions, and sign attesting to its accuracy and completeness. She did so:

I, Sarah Baker, have reviewed the above section titled "Statement of Sarah Baker" and it is true, accurate, and complete.

Signature: *Sarah H. Baker* **Date:** *Sept. 7, YR-1.*

Search of Ashgate Home

At 1115 hours I contacted the on-call DA, Amara Okeke, and informed her that our department needed to conduct additional investigation and that we would need search warrants for Sarah Baker's home and cell phone. I explained the potential involvement of Johnson. Ms. Okeke said this appeared to create a conflict for her office, and she was going to call the attorney general's office and ask them to handle the matter. She said someone from the AG's office would call. I received a call at 1125 hours from Lonnie Voiselle of the AG's office, who agreed to assist our office in obtaining search warrants. Search warrant affidavits were prepared and presented to Magistrate Judge McClintock, who issued both warrants at 1320 hours. I then contacted forensic investigator Dannie Rodriguez of the Darrow County crime laboratory, who agreed to accompany me to the crime scene. Rodriguez and I arrived at Ashgate at 1345 hours where were greeted by Deputy Camelli, who had secured and remained on scene since the events earlier that day.

After putting on gloves and shoe covers, I began by searching the upstairs bedroom in the north wing where Ms. Baker had gone to change her shoes. I did not see any blood in any of the hallways, on the stairs, or in the bedroom. There on top of a closet shelf I found one gun, a fully loaded .38-caliber Smith and Wesson revolver, and a box of .38 ammunition. I also found a box of 9mm ammunition that read 100 rounds but contained 86 rounds. The top of the box was closed. I took custody of the .38 revolver and the ammunition and placed them in an evidence bag. In a desk in the corner of the room I found personal effects including identification documents (Sarah Baker's social security card, birth certificate, and passport) as well as stationery, jewelry, and perfume. I also found a document entitled, "Last Will and Testament of Sarah H. Baker." In reviewing the document, I noticed that Kelly Baker was still listed as the principal beneficiary. I placed this document in an evidence envelope.

Rodriguez and I then went to another large upstairs bedroom in the south wing where we located clothing and articles of property belonging to Kelly Baker, including his wallet with his driver's license on the dresser. We did not see any blood in this room or locate any weapons or ammunition. There was an empty bottle of whiskey and a glass on a night table that appeared to have traces of whiskey in it. On a pillow on the bed, we found an electronic tablet. I photographed the tablet as I found it (Exhibit 11). I then touched the screen and the tablet "woke up." I did not need to enter a passcode. I opened the "Notes" application and immediately saw an open note from September 6th at 10:00pm that said:

Proof that bitch is cheating

- With DA ALL THE TIME on "project"
- Seen in unprofessional settings—owner's box, intimate restaurant, OUR HOME AT NIGHT!
- Wants to cut me out of the will

PLAN OF ACTION:

- Retain Divorces R'Us, hire private investigator to get more evidence of cheating, gather witnesses, make sure Spanalski and Manville are subpoenaed to testify in divorce court about what they have seen and heard going on behind my back.
- TAKE HER FOR ALL SHE'S WORTH!!!!

I took a picture of this note as evidence (Exhibit 12). I then looked through the rest of the "Notes" in the application. There were many, but none appeared relevant to this investigation as they all appeared related to Mr. Baker's work as a news anchor and the stories he was reporting on.

I then looked at the search history on the tablet and saw that the most-recent internet search made was, "How did OJ Simpson get caught?" The timestamp on the search said, "This Morning—Sept. 7th." I know from recent training that this is a law enforcement downside of newly updated privacy protections: we get a date, but not a time. I searched the rest of the internet history on the tablet and uncovered the following searches pertinent to my investigation:

How did OJ Simpson get caught?—*This morning - Sept. 7th*
What's the best proof of cheating in court?—*1 week ago*
How much money can you get without a prenup?—*2 weeks ago*
Is cheating a factor in calculating alimony?—*2 weeks ago*
Who is the best divorce attorney in Nita?—*3 weeks ago*
Nita divorce law—fault or no fault?—*3 weeks ago*
How to tell if your wife is cheating?—*2 months ago*
Kendall Johnson Picture—*2 months ago*
Kendall Johnson D.A. Nita—*2 months ago*
WEB Project—*2 months ago*

I photographed the search history (Exhibit 13). Rodriguez and I then went to the kitchen.

Rodriguez began taking measurements of the area where the body was located, where the kitchen chair and table were, the area where the casings and the gun were found, and areas where blood was located on the floor. Rodriguez pointed out what appeared to be a blood spatter on the east kitchen wall and some bloodstains on the chair. Rodriguez took photographs and samples of blood from the floor, the wall, and the chair and turned over custody of those samples to me for safekeeping. Rodriguez also extracted two bullets from the east wall, placed them in evidence envelopes, and turned them over to me for safekeeping.

The kitchen table had a small plate with a partially eaten croissant and there was a half-empty coffee mug next to it. I took custody of the plate and the mug for possible fingerprint analysis. There was a dish towel next to the sink with what appeared to be a small amount of blood. I photographed and seized it as evidence for later analysis.

I noticed there was an Amazing Alex virtual assistant in the corner of the kitchen next to the stove. I know from my training and experience that these devices can sometimes record conversations that occur in their vicinity, so I seized the Alex and will ask the district court to subpoena Amazing for any recordings it may contain from the morning of September 7, YR-1.

Interview of Chris Spanalski

At 1550 hours Forensic Scientist Rodriguez and I drove to the home of Chris Spanalski, which is located on the grounds of Ashgate Farm on Springs Road. Spanalski agreed to speak with me and tell me what they knew of the shooting. Spanalski said that around 8:30 a.m. Sarah Baker called and said that something terrible had happened and asked them to immediately come to the Ashgate residence. Spanalski's home is about a quarter of a mile away. Spanalski immediately ran over and found Sarah Baker standing on the front porch. She was shaking uncontrollably and crying. Spanalski said that the two walked into the home and Sarah pointed to the kitchen and said, "He's in there. He's dead." Spanalski walked into the kitchen and saw Kelly Baker lying on the floor. There was blood everywhere in the kitchen and on Sarah. Spanalski saw Sarah was bleeding from her arm and asked Sarah, "What happened?" Sarah said that Kelly was drunk and raging and tried to kill her with a knife, and she had to use the gun to defend herself. I asked if Sarah had provided any other details and Spanalski said no and that she was so shaken up and crying and hysterical that she was barely forming complete sentences. Spanalski said it took a while to calm her down to the point where she could speak because she was so hysterical.

Spanalski expressed care for Sarah and was worried about her and didn't know whether Kelly was dead. They told Sarah to calm down and that she had to call 911 immediately. Sarah said she would do that, and Sarah placed the call. I asked Spanalski how much time passed from the time they entered the house to when Sarah called 911, and they said about five minutes. I asked if Spanalski saw any other weapons. Spanalski said only a knife in Kelly's hand, but they did not look closely as they were standing in the doorway by the dining room and they were too shocked by the bloody scene and the confusion.

I asked Spanalski what other information they could offer, and they said only that Sarah is a kind and peaceful person, and she would only have shot Kelly if she truly believed she was going to be hurt or killed. Spanalski had seen Kelly get aggressive before, especially when he's drunk. Spanalski said Kelly is a mean drunk, but they had never seen Sarah act aggressively in response. She usually just tells him to calm down and walks away. She is the type of person who deescalates tense situations, she does not escalate them, so she must have been fighting for her life.

Search of Sarah Baker's Cellphone

On returning to the Detective Division, I retrieved Sarah Baker's cellphone from the property room and proceeded to search it pursuant to the warrant. Of relevance, I found:

- Text messages between Sarah Baker and Kendall Johnson (Exhibit 15).
- Text messages between Sarah Baker and Kelly Baker (Exhibit 16).
- Email with attachment from Kendall Johnson to Sarah Baker (Exhibit 17).
- Sarah Baker's call log for the month of September YR-1 (Exhibit 18).

I then went to the coroner's office, and, with the assistance of Dr. Kahn, I obtained a blood sample and inked fingerprints from the body of Kelly Baker and Kelly Baker's robe and pajamas.

I retained all evidence for safekeeping, and when I completed my investigation on September 7th, I numbered each item of evidence I had obtained and placed each in the department's secure evidence room. The items that I booked for safekeeping were marked and are listed on the evidence sheet at the end of this report.

Recontact with Sarah Baker at County Jail

In light of the evidence recovered in the searches and the delay in Sarah Baker's calling 911, I decided to talk further with Sarah Baker. At approximately 1700 hours I returned to the Darrow County Jail and asked to speak with Ms. Baker. The jailer brought Ms. Baker to the interview room. I explained that I wanted to ask some follow-up questions concerning evidence that I had located at her home, cell phone, and what appeared to be a delay in making the 911 call. Ms. Baker informed me that she had spoken with her attorney, who had advised her that she should not discuss the case further with law enforcement, and, therefore, she was unable to talk with me.

Interview of Kendall Johnson

At approximately 1730 hours I called Kendall Johnson, the chief deputy district attorney of Darrow County, and informed Johnson of my role in the investigation and asked Johnson to meet with me at the sheriff's department. Johnson agreed.

At 1750 hours Johnson arrived at the station, and we spoke in my office. I informed Johnson of our investigation into the death of Kelly Baker. Johnson was aware of Mr. Baker's death—initially from district attorney Amara Okeke, and then others talking about it at the DA's office. I told Johnson that Sarah Baker had been booked for homicide, and that the attorney general's office was handling the prosecution. I said their relationship was a matter of importance and that we needed to talk about that relationship. Johnson agreed to cooperate.

Johnson said the relationship with Sarah Baker was purely professional and stems from their working together to create a Center for Battered Women through Project WEB and the Darrow County Battered Women Council. Johnson said there were numerous occasions when the two had to meet to work on plans for the center. Those meetings took place at Project WEB, the meeting room of the council, and, on occasion, Ashgate. Johnson did not recall ever being completely alone with Sarah at Ashgate and couldn't remember the two of them eating alone at a restaurant. I asked Johnson how they would communicate. Johnson said via text, email, calls, and in-person meetings, but they were always strictly professional. I then showed Johnson the birthday text message I found in Sarah's phone and asked whether they had sent it. Johnson paused for about ten seconds and then said, "Well, I forgot about that. But it was just a sweet message to help make Sarah smile on her birthday." I also showed Johnson some of the other texts and specifically asked what, "I know this is a tough grind, but we just have to get through it" meant. Johnson said the tough process of getting the Center approved and funded. Johnson knew that at times it was discouraging for Sarah because she was not used to this kind of bureaucratic process.

I asked Johnson to let me know if there was any additional information that might be relevant to our investigation. Johnson agreed. They then asked to what extent my department intended to release information to the press about the relationship with Sarah. I told Johnson it was not up to me, and to talk with Sheriff Litwhiler, who handled the press releases.

Request for Fingerprint Examination

At 0830 hours on September 8, YR-1, I called Senior I.D. Technician Robin Mulligan of our department and requested that Mulligan examine Items #1–34 to determine whether the items contained fingerprints and conduct comparison testing of the same. I informed Mulligan that Investigator Rodriguez would be conducting a full forensic examination of the same items and, therefore, requested a speedy conclusion to Mulligan's examination so items #1–34 could then be transferred to Rodriguez.

Mulligan agreed to come to the detective division immediately. At 0840 hours I turned over to Mulligan items of evidence #1–34. At the completion of Mulligan's testing, I collected the items back and turned them over to Dannie Rodriguez for further testing. Rodriguez later returned the items to me when that testing was completed.

Interview of Kit Manville

At 0950 hours on September 8, YR-1, I called Chris Spanalski and asked if the employment records revealed any employees at Ashgate Farm with the first name of "Kit." Spanalski informed me that for a period of two years Ashgate employed Kit Manville as a farrier. Spanalski said that Manville was terminated on September 1, YR-1, after Spanalski conferred with Sarah Baker, for "lack of competence and dependability." Spanalski said that Manville was not punctual and did not complete shoeing jobs on time. They said that Manville was given three months' severance pay. Spanalski said that Manville was capable of doing very good work, and Manville was an asset as an entertainer when they had parties, but Manville had a big problem with "the bottle." Manville was kept on because Mr. Baker and Manville were friendly—they liked to drink and gamble on horses together. In fact, Spanalski said there were rumors that the two of them had gotten into some trouble down at the tracks with the amount of money they owed some bookies. Eventually Manville's drinking problem got too severe, and Manville had to be discharged.

I asked Spanalski for Manville's address and phone number. Spanalski informed me that Manville lived at 19925 Talbot Road in the county and gave me Manville's phone number. I then phoned Manville and arranged to go to Manville's home for an interview.

At 1140 hours on September 8, YR-1, I drove to Manville's residence. Manville informed me that they had been employed by Ashgate Farm as a farrier for about two years. Manville had extensive experience as a farrier at a different farm, Barrett Farm, in Nita. Manville was recruited with the promise of more pay and more side opportunities to provide singing entertainment for Ashgate parties. Manville has for a number of years sung and played guitar for upscale parties. Manville first met with Chris Spanalski, and after Spanalski made the decision to hire Manville, then they met with Ms. Baker and were hired.

Manville said problems began when they had the misfortune to witness an incident involving Ms. Baker. Manville said that a customer named Will White bought a polo pony from Ashgate Farm and later the pony died. White thought that Ashgate knew or should have known of the illness, and when Ashgate claimed the pony was fine when sold, White became angry. Manville said White talked with Spanalski about the problem, and Spanalski said they were not responsible. Apparently White then asked who Spanalski's boss was, and Spanalski said that Ms. Baker owned Ashgate Farm. White came by in the evening about 7:00 p.m. and apparently couldn't find anyone. Manville happened to be completing some work and talked with White. White said that he left messages for Ms. Baker and she would not return his calls, so he came by to talk to her. He asked where her home was, and Manville indicated it was down the road. White walked down to the house, and Manville walked along to make sure everything was all right. He saw them talking on the porch, and then Ms. Baker yelled for him to leave. White walked down from the porch and stood at the bottom of the steps and said something about suing Ms. Baker. He said Ms. Baker again yelled for him to leave and then went into the house. She came out about one minute later with a gun in her hand. She pointed it up in the air and yelled, "You get out of here now, unless you want to be carried out!" Without another word, she began firing the gun in the air. White ran to his car and left.

Ms. Baker came down the steps to Manville and said, "You saw what he did. He tried to attack me." Manville just gave a shrug of the shoulders, and Ms. Baker went back into the house. Apparently White called the sheriff, because about an hour later two deputies arrived. They saw Manville working and asked what Manville saw. Manville repeated to the deputies what happened. About one week later, Ms. Baker's lawyer called Manville and said that she understood Manville was going to be a witness for the prosecution. Manville told the attorney the same thing they told the sheriffs and said that was all they knew. Manville denied drinking alcohol that day at work and only had a drink after going home that evening.

Manville said that Mr. Baker was a great guy and that they were good friends. They liked to have a good time together, and even though Mr. Baker had paid off some of Manville's gambling debts, Manville didn't feel like he owed Mr. Baker anything and "definitely wouldn't lie to protect him." Mr. Baker would come home some evenings, and if Manville was still working at the farm, they would talk and sometimes have a beer. Sometime several months ago, Manville began to think that Ms. Baker was getting pretty cozy with someone who was always coming to the house for "meetings." This bothered Manville, because Mr. Baker was never there when this happened. One evening Mr. Baker came home, and apparently Ms. Baker was gone. He came over to Manville, and they had a beer or two. After talking for a while, Manville decided to see if Mr. Baker knew anything about this new person, so they mentioned the meetings. Manville said that Mr. Baker said he was sure it was just business dealings with the battered women project.

Then one evening around 6:30 p.m. Manville saw Ms. Baker and another person get out of Ms. Baker's Lexus and walk to the front porch. Manville heard Ms. Baker say something like, "Oh, Kendall, I love the things you say to me." Then Ms. Baker put her head on the person's shoulder and just laughed. They walked into the house. Mr. Baker must have been working late because he didn't come home while Manville watched. Manville said the two then came out of the house about an hour later. They got in her Lexus and drove off.

About a week later, Manville was at the farm office and heard Ms. Baker and Chris Spanalski talking. Manville heard Ms. Baker say, "I've decided to cut Kelly out of the will." The next day, Manville called Kelly Baker and told him what had happened. Apparently, Kelly Baker was shocked, because there was a long pause, and then Kelly Baker said, "You're a true friend, and I won't forget it."

Shortly after that, Chris Spanalski gave Manville a termination notice with three months' severance pay. That was the last Manville heard about the matter until the news broke on TV that Kelly Baker had been murdered and his wife had been arrested. Manville said that Sarah Baker must have murdered him to get him out of the way because Ms. Baker "always gets what she wants." Manville was "annoyed and upset" that Ms. Baker would let them go and thought the termination was a "big sham" just to punish them. Manville "hoped that Ms. Baker rotted in jail." Manville admitted that in years past they had abused alcohol and gotten in trouble for it.

Review of Criminal Records on Kelly Baker and Sarah Baker

I ran automated criminal records checks on Kelly Baker and Sarah Baker. I found two police entries for Kelly Baker, a battery arrest and a DUI, both in YR-6. I found one sheriff's entry for Sarah Baker, a citation for CC 12031 in YR-2. I contacted the police and sheriff's records custodians and obtained official copies for each offense and have attached them to this report.

Items of Physical Evidence Collected for Forensics Examination (see reports from Dannie Rodriguez and Robin Mulligan for DNA and fingerprint analysis and results)

Item 1 One 9mm Luger semiautomatic pistol, serial #6851

Item 2 One butcher knife

Item 3 Two 9mm cartridge cases

Item 4 One 9mm cartridge case

Item 5 One 9mm cartridge case

Item 6 Four 9mm cartridges, 6a from chamber and 6b, 6c, and 6d from magazine

Item 7 Six .38-caliber cartridges

Item 8 One .38-caliber Smith and Wesson revolver

Item 9 One pair of white canvas shoes

Item 10 One hair sample from Sarah Baker

Item 11 One sealed vial of blood from Sarah Baker

Item 12 One pair of pants from Sarah Baker

Item 13 One blouse from Sarah Baker

Item 14a One blood sample from the kitchen floor in front of the sink

Item 14b One blood sample from kitchen floor where Kelly Baker's body was found

Item 15 One blood sample from the kitchen wall

Item 16 One blood sample from the kitchen chair

Item 17 One coffee mug from the kitchen table

Item 18 One plate from the kitchen table

Item 19 One dish towel from kitchen counter near sink

Item 20 One document entitled, "Last Will and Testament of Sarah Baker"

Item 21 One electronic tablet from upstairs bedroom

Item 22 One glass from upstairs bedroom

Item 23 One whiskey bottle from upstairs bedroom

Item 24 One box of 9mm ammunition

Item 25 One box of .38-caliber ammunition

Item 26 Inked fingerprints of Sarah Baker

Item 27 Inked fingerprints of Kelly Baker

Item 28 One sealed vial of blood from Kelly Baker

Item 29 One men's robe from Kelly Baker

Item 30 One pair of men's pajamas from Kelly Baker

Item 31 One 9mm bullet from wound #1 received from Dr. Kahn

Item 32 One 9mm bullet from wound #3 received from Dr. Kahn

Item 33 One 9mm bullet from kitchen wall 31" high received from Dannie Rodriguez

Item 34 One 9mm bullet from kitchen wall 33" high received from Dannie Rodriguez

IN THE DISTRICT COURT
OF THE STATE OF NITA
COUNTY OF DARROW

THE STATE OF NITA	)	
	)	SW-CC187-1
In re Sarah Baker	)	
	)	

Search Warrant: Suspect's Residence

To: Det. Lee of the Darrow County Sheriff's Dept.

You are hereby commanded in the name of the State of Nita to forthwith search either in day or night the residence at 8714 Springs Road, Warrenton, Nita, described as a single-family dwelling of white brick and stone construction on Springs Road off Route 211 in Darrow County, for any knives, firearms and ammunition (including any such items already seized for safety reasons), blood, fingerprints, documents, correspondence, financial statements, clothing (including clothing already seized from the suspect upon arrest), and/or electronics that in any way relate to the death of Kelly Baker and take any necessary photographs, measurements, and diagrams.

You are further commanded to seize said property, person, and/or objects if they are found and to produce before this court an inventory of all property, persons, and/or objects seized during this authorized search.

This search warrant is issued in relation to an offense substantially described as follows:

The homicide of Kelly Baker in violation of Section 100 of N.C.C. I, the undersigned, have found probable cause to believe that the property or person constitutes evidence of the crime identified herein or tends to show that the person(s) named or described herein has committed or is committing a crime and further that the search should be made, based on the statements in the attached affidavit sworn to by

Casey Lee
Name of Affiant

Kevin McClintock
Magistrate

Date: September 7, YR-1

IN THE DISTRICT COURT
OF THE STATE OF NITA
COUNTY OF DARROW

THE STATE OF NITA	)	
	)	SW-CC187-1
In re Sarah Baker	)	
	)	

Search Warrant Inventory and Return: Suspect's Residence

The following items were seized following a search of the suspect's residence under authority of warrant:

1. One Smith and Wesson .38-caliber revolver.
2. One box .38-caliber ammunition.
3. One box 9mm Luger ammunition.
4. One Last Will and Testament of Sarah Baker.
5. One electronic tablet from upstairs bedroom.
6. One whiskey bottle from upstairs bedroom.
7. One glass from upstairs bedroom.
8. Measurements from the kitchen.
9. One blood swab from the chair in the kitchen.
10. One blood swab from the wall in the kitchen.
11. One blood swab from the floor in front of the kitchen sink.
12. One blood swab from the floor in the kitchen where Kelly Baker's body was found.
13. One coffee mug from the kitchen table.
14. One plate from the kitchen table.
15. One dish towel from the kitchen counter.
16. Two bullets from east wall of the kitchen.
17. One Amazing Alex.

The statement above is true and accurate to the best of my knowledge and belief.

Casey Lee

Executing Officer

Kevin McClintock

Magistrate

Date: September 7, YR-1

Exhibit 10

LAST WILL AND TESTAMENT OF SARAH BAKER

I, Sarah Hanna Baker, a resident of the County of Darrow, State of Nita, declare that this is my last will.

FIRST: I revoke all former wills and codicils to wills.

SECOND: Kelly Baker, my husband, is living. I have no children or issue of any deceased child.

THIRD: I have not entered into a contract to make a will or a contract not to revoke a will.

FOURTH: If my husband survives me by thirty days, I give all my property to him except for the residence and land located at 8718 Springs Road in Warrenton.

FIFTH: If my husband does not survive me by thirty days, I give all of my property to my father, Elton Martin, except for the residence and land located at 8718 Springs Road in Warrenton.

SIXTH: I give the residence and land located at 8718 Springs Road in Warrenton to Chris Spanalski, the manager of Ashgate Farm.

SEVENTH: I appoint my husband executor of this will, to serve without bond; and, if he fails or ceases to act, I appoint my father, Elton Martin, as the executor of this will, to serve without bond.

EIGHTH: I authorize my executor, with or without notice, to sell at either public or private sale all property belonging to my estate, subject only to such confirmation of court as may be required by law.

NINTH: If any beneficiary under this will directly or indirectly contests or attacks this will or any provision thereof, the gift to that beneficiary is revoked, and the property that would have been given to that beneficiary shall be distributed as though that beneficiary had predeceased me without issue.

IN WITNESS WHEREOF, I have subscribed this will, consisting of these two pages, at the end thereof on this 24th day of March, YR-5.

Signature of Testator: *Sarah Hanna Baker*

Subscribing Witnesses: *Lisa Williams*

Ashley S. Patterson

On this date and in our presence, Sarah H. Baker, the testatrix, personally subscribed her name at the end of the foregoing instrument, at which she declared to us, as attesting witnesses, that it was her will; at the request of the testatrix and in her presence and in the presence of each other, we have subscribed our names as witnesses to her will; at that time, the testatrix was over eighteen years of age and appeared to be of sound mind; we have no knowledge of any facts indicating that the instrument, or any part of it, was procured by duress, menace, fraud, or undue influence.

We, individually, certify under penalty of perjury that the foregoing is true and correct. Executed on this 24th day of March, YR-5, at Nita City, Nita.

Lisa Williams residing at 1142 High Street, Nita City, Nita

Ashley S. Patterson residing at 302 Greenup Street, Nita City, Nita

Exhibit 11

Tablet Found on Kelly Baker's Bed

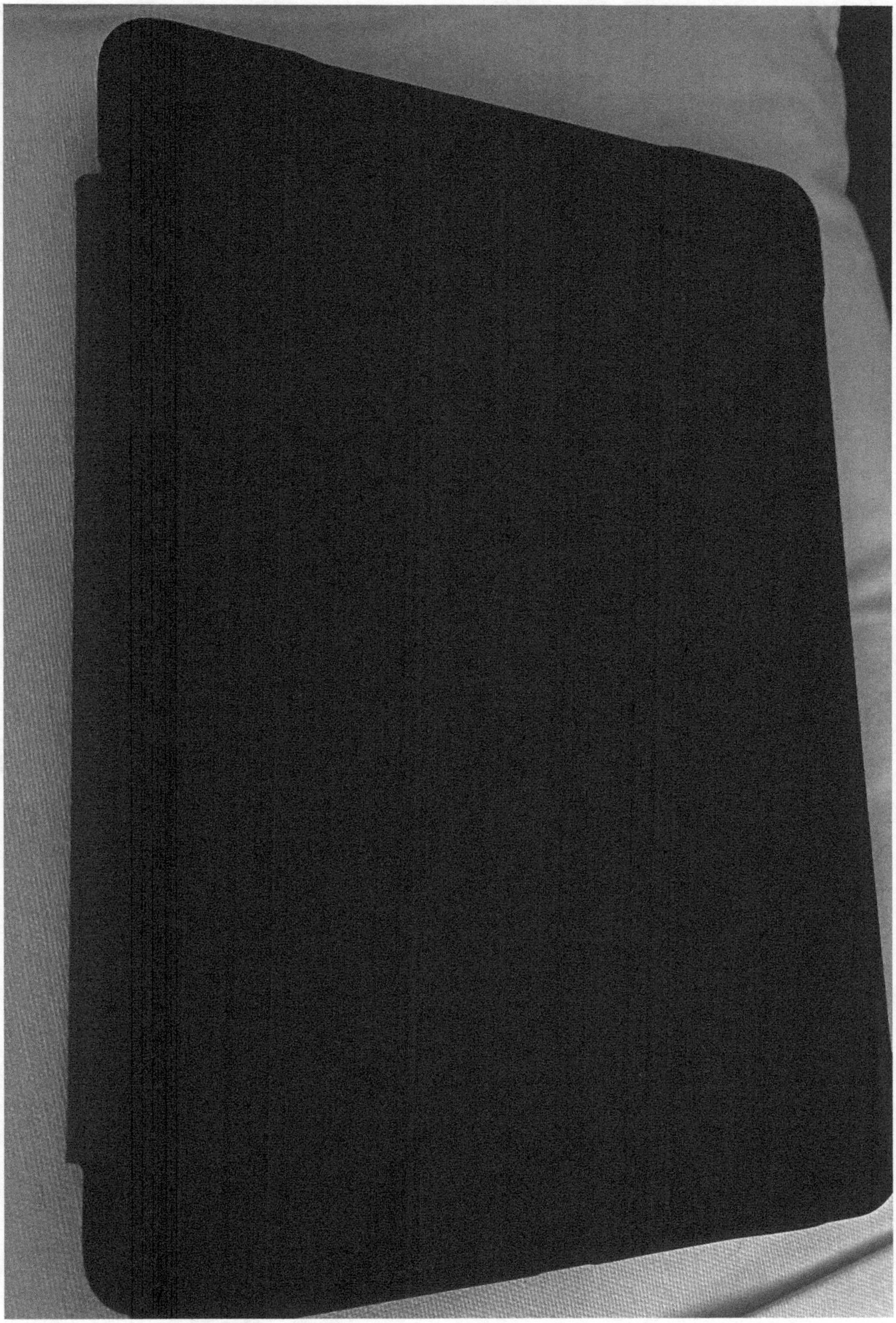

Exhibit 12

Note Found in Kelly Baker's Tablet

< Notes

Sept. 6th - 10:00pm

Proof that bitch is cheating

- With DA ALL THE TIME on "project"
- Seen in unprofessional settings - owner's box, intimate restaurant, OUR HOME AT NIGHT!
- Wants to cut me out of the will

PLAN OF ACTION:

- Retain Divorces R'Us, hire private investigator to get more evidence of cheating, gather witnesses, make sure Spanalski and Manville are subpoenaed to testify in divorce court about what they have seen and heard going on behind my back.
- TAKE HER FOR ALL SHE'S WORTH!!!

Exhibit 13

Search History Found in Kelly Baker's Tablet

Recent Searches

- How did OJ Simpson get caught? – *This morning - Sept. 7th*
- What's the best proof of cheating in court? – *1 week ago*
- How much money can you get without a prenup? – *2 weeks ago*
- Is cheating a factor in calculating alimony? – *2 weeks ago*
- Who is the best divorce attorney in Nita? – *3 weeks ago*
- Nita divorce law – fault or no fault? – *3 weeks ago*
- How to tell if your wife is cheating? – *2 months ago*
- Kendall Johnson Picture – *2 months ago*
- Kendall Johnson D.A. Nita – *2 months ago*
- WEB Project – *2 months ago*

Exhibit 14

Whiskey Bottle and Glass Found in Kelly Baker's Room

IN THE DISTRICT COURT
OF THE STATE OF NITA
COUNTY OF DARROW

THE STATE OF NITA	)	
	)	SW-CC187-2
In re Sarah Baker	)	
	)	

Search Warrant: Suspect's Cell Phone

To: Det. Lee of the Darrow County Sheriff's Dept.

You are hereby commanded in the name of the State of Nita to forthwith search either in day or night the cell phone belonging to Sarah Baker, and currently in the possession of the Darrow County Sheriff's Dept. following her arrest, for any communications, including but not limited to text messages, emails, call logs/history, and/or other electronically stored evidence on the device in any way relating to the death of Kelly Baker.

You are further commanded to seize said evidence if it is found and to produce before this court an inventory of the same.

This search warrant is issued in relation to an offense substantially described as follows:

The homicide of Kelly Baker in violation of Section 100 of N.C.C. I, the undersigned, have found probable cause to believe that the property or person constitutes evidence of the crime identified herein or tends to show that the person(s) named or described herein has committed or is committing a crime and further that the search should be made, based on the statements in the attached affidavit sworn to by

Casey Lee
Name of Affiant

Kevin McClintock
Magistrate

Date: September 7, YR-1

IN THE DISTRICT COURT
OF THE STATE OF NITA
COUNTY OF DARROW

THE STATE OF NITA	)	
	)	SW-CC187-2
In re Sarah Baker	)	
	)	

Search Warrant Inventory and Return: Suspect's Cell Phone

The following items, and no others, were seized under authority of this warrant:

1. Text messages between Sarah Baker and Kendall Johnson.
2. Text messages between Sarah Baker and Kelly Baker.
3. Email from Kendall Johnson to Sarah Baker.
4. Sarah Baker's call log for the month of September YR-1.

The statement above is true and accurate to the best of my knowledge and belief.

Casey Lee
Executing Officer

Kevin McClintock
Magistrate

Date: September 7, YR-1

Exhibit 15

Text Messages Between Sarah Baker and Kendall Johnson

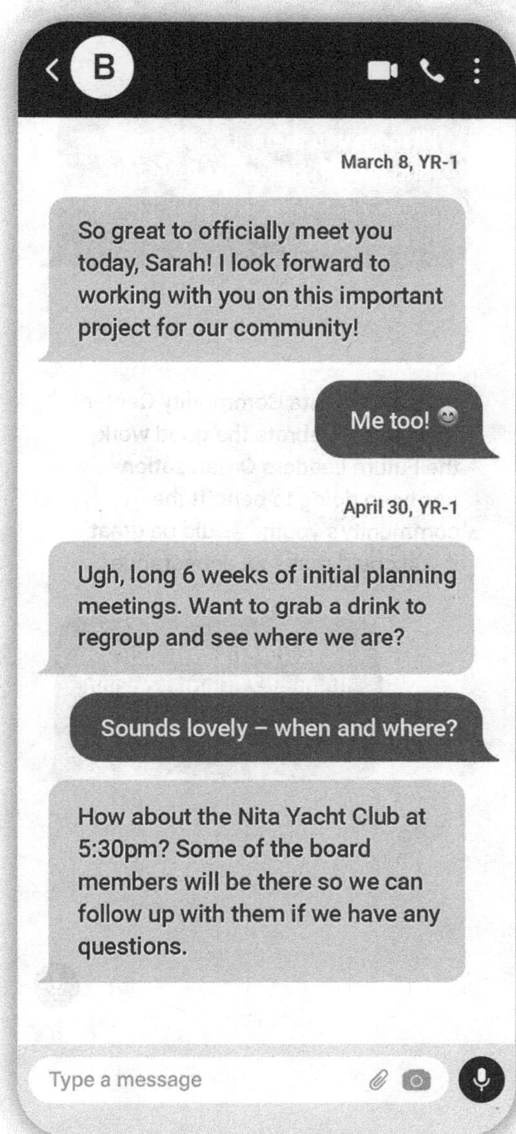

Exhibit 15 (cont.)

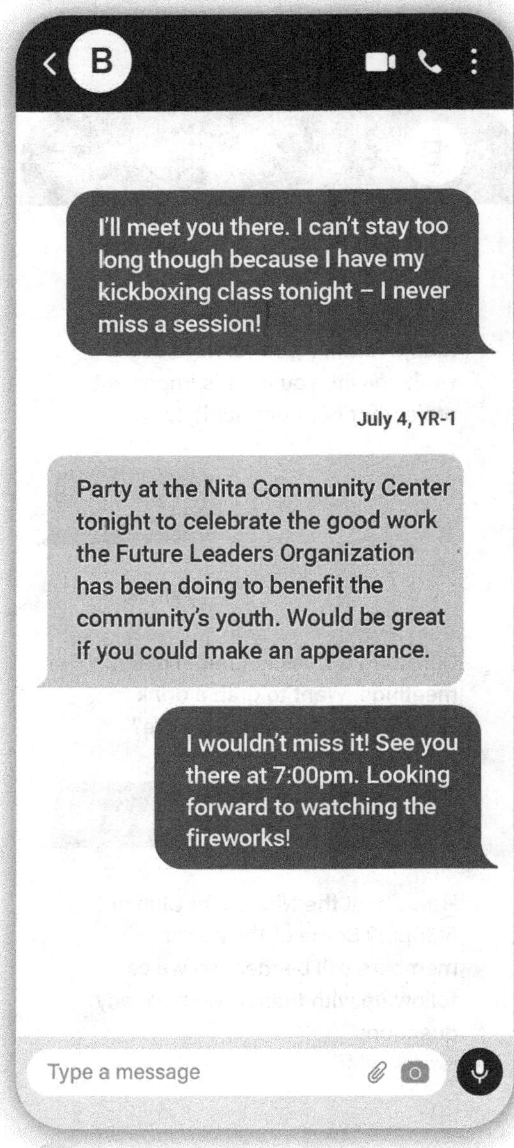

Exhibit 15 (cont.)

Exhibit 15 (cont.)

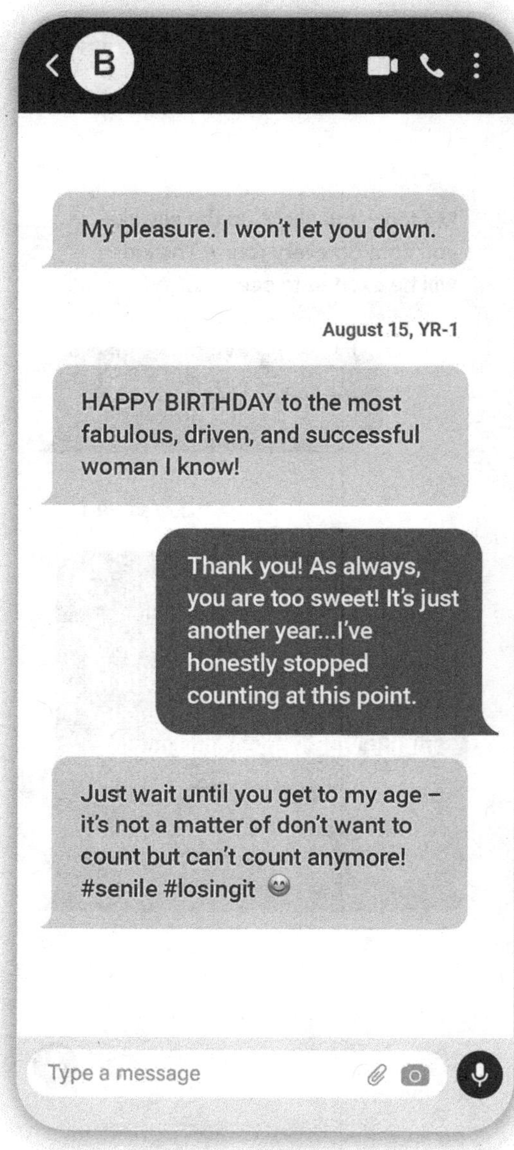

Exhibit 15 (cont.)

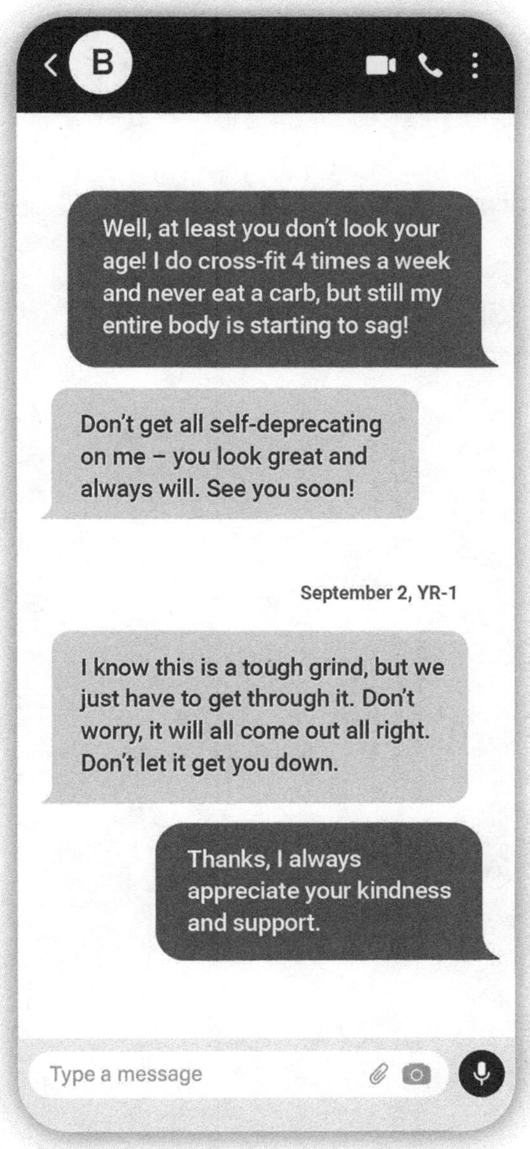

Exhibit 16

Text Messages Between Sarah Baker and Kelly Baker

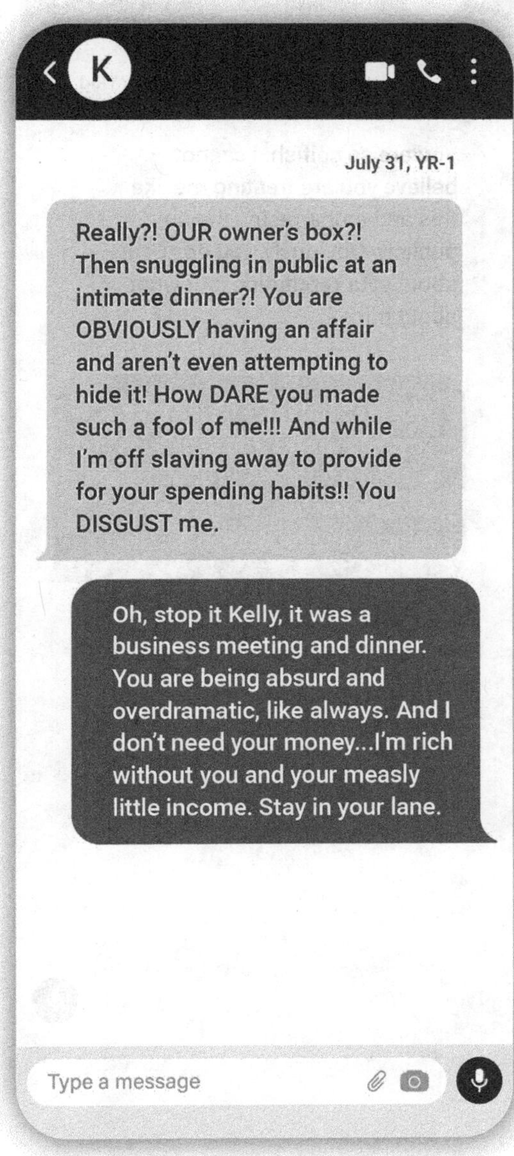

Exhibit 16 (cont.)

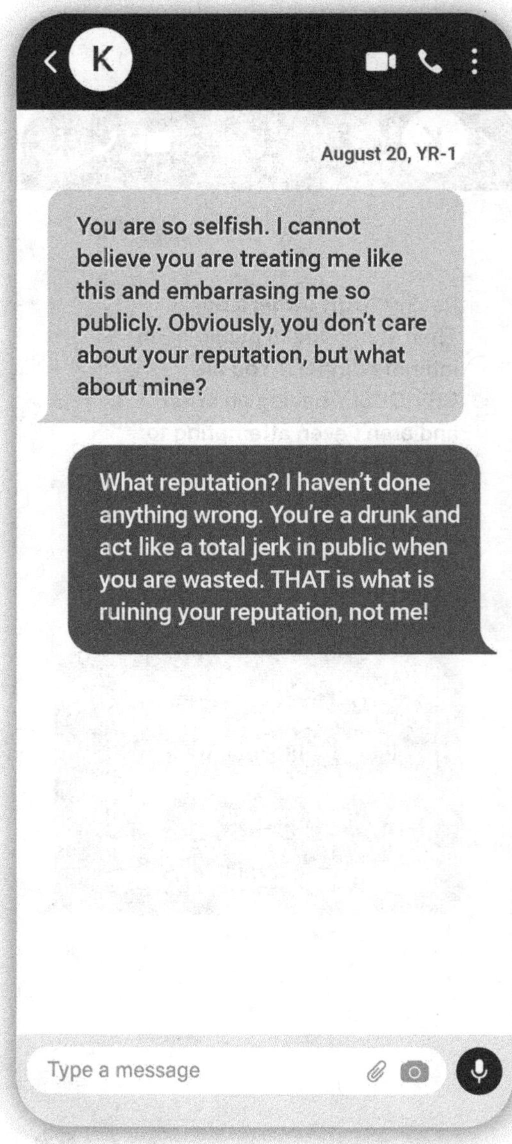

Exhibit 16 (cont.)

Exhibit 17

Email with Attachment from Kendall Johnson to Sarah Baker

Sarah Baker

To:	Sarah_Baker@ashgateestate.org
From:	KJohnson@darrowcountyda.gov
Date:	August 7, YR-1
Subject:	A letter for you
Attachments:	baker_appreciation.docx

Sarah,

See attached as requested.

Kendall :)

Exhibit 17 (cont.)

Office of the District Attorney
Darrow County, Nita

Amara Okeke District Attorney
550 Main Street
Nita City, Nita 57815
(819) 555-3849
dcda.gov.nita

August 7, YR-1

Sarah H. Baker
Ashgate Farm
8714 Springs Road
Warrenton, Nita 55060

Dear Ms. Baker:

Your efforts in helping Darrow County develop a center for abused women have inspired volunteers and county workers. It is clear that under your able direction, our county will soon have a state-of-the-art facility to protect abused women and offer them a hope for their future.

Please accept the appreciation of our office and all the county agencies serving in Project WEB for the work you have done thus far and keep our appreciation in mind as we enter the final development stages of this vast and important project.

Sincerely,

Kendall
Kendall Johnson

Lonnie Voiselle

Ella Marie Wright, Attorney General

By Lonnie Voiselle, Deputy Attorney General

Exhibit 18

Sarah Baker's Call Log for the Month of September YR-1

SEPTEMBER 1, YR-1
7:30PM: KELLY BAKER—INCOMING
30 SECONDS

SEPTEMBER 2, YR-1
9:30AM: DARROW COUNTY DISTRICT ATTORNEY'S OFFICE—OUTGOING
90 MINUTES

12:00PM: GLAMOUR SALON & SPA—OUTGOING
3 MINUTES, 25 SECONDS

4:00PM: CHRIS SPANALSKI—INCOMING
10 MINUTES

SEPTEMBER 3, YR-1
11:00AM: WEB PROJECT MANAGER BILL KAZANSKI—INCOMING
30 MINUTES

3:30PM: DARROW COUNTY DISTRICT ATTORNEY'S OFFICE—INCOMING
5 MINUTES

SEPTEMBER 4, YR-1
9:00AM: ORANGE THEORY FITNESS—OUTGOING
5 MINUTES

1:00PM: DARROW COUNTY DISTRICT ATTORNEY'S OFFICE—INCOMING
20 MINUTES

4:00PM: WEB PROJECT MANAGER BILL KAZANSKI—OUTGOING
1 HOUR

SEPTEMBER 6, YR-1
10:00AM: DARROW COUNTY DISTRICT ATTORNEY'S OFFICE—OUTGOING
45 MINUTES

2:00PM: PLUSH & PINK NAIL SALON—OUTGOING
2 MINUTES

5:30PM: KELLY BAKER—INCOMING
30 SECONDS

SEPTEMBER 7, YR-1
8:27AM: CHRIS SPANALSKI—OUTGOING CALL—30 SECONDS

SUBPOENA

THE STATE OF NITA COUNTY OF DARROW In re Sarah Baker	))))	SUB-CC187-1

TO: Amazing Inc. c/o Office of Corporation Counsel

You are hereby required to produce any and all Amazing Alex recordings by Device # 1103001923 registered to Sarah Baker and/or Kelly Baker between the hours of 7:30am and 9:30am EST on September 7, YR-1 to be used as evidence by the Prosecution or Defense in a murder case pending before the Darrow County District Court.

By agreement and stipulation of the parties, a custodian of records does not need to appear in person. In lieu of in-person testimony, the custodian of records may provide an affidavit as to the circumstances, completeness, and authenticity of any recording downloaded and turned over as evidence in accordance with this lawful subpoena.

Herein fail not under penalty of law.

Witness The Honorable Kevin McClintock, Magistrate Judge of said Court, this September 8, YR-1.

Madeline S. Goldberg

Madeline S. Goldberg
Clerk of the District Court
Darrow County, Nita

Exhibit 19

Cover Letter and Affidavit from Amazing Custodian of Electronic Records

Amazing Inc.
"We've got you covered—We're Amazing!"

Dear Ms. Goldberg,

Amazing, Inc. is in receipt of your subpoena regarding the matter of In Re Sarah Baker, Case No. SW-106–YR-1. In lawful compliance with said subpoena, Amazing's custodian of electronic records, Mr. Paul Jensen, has provided the attached affidavit. I have also provided the subpoenaed recording. I trust this concludes Amazing's involvement with this matter.

Regards,

Ira Lowell

Ira Lowell, Esq.
Chief Corporation Counsel
Amazing, Inc.

Exhibit 19 (cont.)

AFFIDAVIT

On this 17th day of September YR-1, for the purpose of complying with a lawful subpoena issued by the District Court of Darrow County in the State of Nita, the undersigned, Custodian of Electronic Records for Amazing, Inc., does solemnly swear and affirm under penalty of perjury that the only recording made by Device # 1103001923 (registered to Sarah Baker) between the hours of 7:30am and 9:30am EST on September 7, YR-1, was secured and turned over to the lawful authority of the City of Nita, Darrow County.

The recording started at 8:15am and lasted 13 seconds. The undersigned further affirms under penalty of perjury that there is no way for a customer to alter, change, or delete any portion of a recording from the device. Alex virtual assistants are not designed to record all the time, but a software-design flaw has been identified indicating that they can, but do not always, begin to record when voices rise. There is no consistent time period through which they will continue to record, and our design team has been unable to determine why they stop recording. In other words, Alex virtual assistants can record certain moments in time, initially triggered by elevated voice volume. We are working to resolve this software issue.

Paul Jensen
Printed Name

September 17, YR-1
Date

Paul Jensen
Signature

ACKNOWLEDGMENT OF NOTARY

Bobbi Brewer
Printed Name

September 17, YR-1
Date

Bobbi Brewer
Signature
Notary Public

Exhibit 20

Amazing Alex Recording
Device 1103001923
Registered to Sarah Baker

(Recording available at http://bit.ly/1P20Jea, password Baker4)

Exhibit 20A

Transcript of Amazing Alex Recording
Device 1103001923
Registered to Sarah Baker

Kelly Baker: Well look who it is, the unfaithful bitch.

Sarah Baker: Oh my god really Kelly? You're acting crazy, this is insane!

Exhibit 21

REPORT OF SENIOR IDENTIFICATION TECHNICIAN ROBIN MULLIGAN

Darrow County Sheriff's Department
Bureau of Identification

Nita City, Nita

Offense Report #YR-1-28088

Report entered: 09/11/YR-1

Incident Type/Offense	Location	Reporting Officer
CC 100—Homicide	Ashgate Farm 8714 Springs Road Warrenton, Nita	Robin Mulligan Senior I.D. Technician
Date/Time Reported	Date/Time Occurred	
9/7/YR-1, 08:51		

Persons		
Role	Name	
Victim	Kelly Lawrence Baker	
Arrestee/Suspect	Sarah Hanna Baker	

DCSD Fingerprint Identification Report

CC 100—Homicide

On September 8, YR-1, at 0830 hours, I received a telephone request from Detective Casey Lee asking that I conduct a fingerprint examination and comparison of evidence seized in the above case. Detective Lee informed me that the evidence would soon be turned over to Forensic Scientist Dannie Rodriguez and asked that I perform my examination as soon as possible. I then went to the sheriff's detective division and at 0845 hours received from Detective Lee the following items.

On September 8, YR-1, at 1030 hours, I conducted my examination of the items of evidence as follows. Based on my training and experience, I only examined items for fingerprints that could have possibly contained fingerprints (clean, flat surfaces—not cloth or paper).

Photographing of Evidence

Before conducting any fingerprint examination, I photographed Item #1, the 9mm Luger pistol, serial #6851, and magazine, and Item 2, the butcher knife.

Item #1—9mm Luger Pistol and Magazine

I examined Item #1 and found it to be a 9mm Luger pistol, serial #6851, with a magazine. I processed Item 1 for prints and was able to find one usable latent on the trigger guard of the pistol, which I lifted and labeled Latent #1. There were other partial prints in the area of the trigger guard and on the clip that appeared smudged and unusable. I then compared Latent #1 with the prints in Items 26 and 27 and was able to find sufficient points of comparison to state that Latent #1 was left by the right index finger of Sarah Baker.

Item #2—The Butcher Knife

I processed this item for prints. After checking both the blade and the handle, I was unable to find any usable prints.

Items #3–9

After checking these items, I was able to find one usable print on the side of Item #6b. As I understand it, this live cartridge was found in the magazine of the 9mm pistol. I labeled this Latent #2 and compared it with the known inked impressions in Items 26 and 27. I was able to positively identify Latent #2 as a print made by the right index finger of Kelly Baker.

I was able to find one usable latent print on Item #8 on the .38-caliber revolver cylinder. I lifted that print and labeled it Latent #5. I then compared it with the known prints in Items 26 and 27 and found it to be the right thumb of Sarah Baker.

Items #17–18

I processed these items for prints. Both items contained multiple sets of smudged prints, but there were insufficient points to make a positive comparison.

Item #21

I processed this item for prints. I was unable to find any usable prints.

Items #22–23

I processed these items for prints and was able to find two usable latent prints on Item #22. I lifted those prints and labeled them Latent #6 and #7. I then compared these with the known prints in Items 26 and 27 and found it to be the right thumb and index finger of Kelly Baker.

I was also able to find one usable latent print on Item #23. I lifted that print and labeled it Latent #8. I then compared it with the known prints in Items #26 and #27 and found it to be the right thumb of Kelly Baker.

Items #24–25

I processed these items for prints and was unable to find any usable prints.

Return of Evidence

I returned Latents #1–#8 to my evidence locker. I then called Det. Lee at approximately 1450 hours on September 8, YR-1, and informed Det. Lee of the results and the detective came to collect all evidence items.

Darrow County Sheriff's Department
Bureau of Identification
Nita City, Nita
Offense Report #YR-1–28088
Report entered: 09/10/YR-1

Incident Type/Offense	Location	Reporting Officer
CC 100—Homicide	Ashgate Farm 8714 Springs Road Warrenton, Nita	Dannie Rodriguez Forensic Scientist
Date/Time Reported	**Date/Time Occurred**	
9/7/YR-1, 08:51		

Persons		
Role	Name	
Victim	Kelly Lawrence Baker	
Arrestee/Suspect	Sarah Hanna Baker	

DCSD Forensic Investigation Report
CC 100—Homicide

Search of Ashgate Farm Residence

On September 7, YR-1, at approximately 1325 hours, Detective Lee informed me that I was needed to assist in a shooting investigation at Ashgate Farm in Warrenton. I met Detective Lee at the station, and we drove to Ashgate Farm, arriving at approximately 1345 hours. Detective Lee had a search warrant for the residence, and we met Deputy Camelli outside, who had secured and remained on scene since the events earlier in the morning. We entered the home and went directly to the upstairs bedroom, which appeared to have been occupied by Sarah Baker. I did not observe any blood in the bedroom, or on the path we walked leading to the bedroom from the front door. Detective Lee located and seized evidence. We then went to the other side of the house—again, I did not see any blood along the way—and searched what appeared to be Kelly Baker's bedroom. I also did not see any blood in this bedroom. Detective Lee photographed an empty whiskey bottle, glass, and electronic tablet, and seized them all as evidence.

We then went to the first-floor kitchen. I did not notice any clear shoe imprints in the blood on the floor, but much of the blood was smeared and disturbed since the body had been checked for vitals by the responding officer, as well as later examined and removed by the coroner. As a result, I was unable to do a shoe-print comparison to determine whether Sarah Baker had walked near Kelly Baker's body after he was dead. I was, however, able to measure distances from the chalk outline of Kelly Baker's body to the kitchen table; chair; the position of the 9mm pistol and the casings; and bloodstains on the floor, chair, and wall. I also measured the height and width of the table and the chair. I took samples of blood from the floor (the area where Kelly Baker's body was found and the separate stain in front of the sink), the chair, and the wall. I placed the items in sealed evidence containers. I retrieved two bullets from the east wall, one at a height of 31" and the other at a height of 33". I placed them in sealed evidence envelopes. I did not see any evidence of blood on the kitchen table. I took pictures of the blood stains on the wall, the chair, and the floor of the kitchen. I noticed a dish towel that was on the counter by the sink that appeared to have some dried blood on it. I seized this towel and placed it in an evidence bag.

After concluding our examination of the residence at Ashgate, Detective Lee and I drove to Chris Spanalski's home, arriving there sometime around 1600 hours. Following our discussion with Spanalski, I turned over to Detective Lee for safekeeping the blood samples and bullets I retrieved from the kitchen area.

Examination of the Body of Kelly Baker

At 1650 hours I went to the Darrow County coroner's office and, in the presence of Dr. Kahn, performed a gunshot residue test on the body of Kelly Baker. I found no traces of gunshot residue anywhere on the body of Kelly Baker.

Preparation of Diagrams

At 0815 hours on September 8, YR-1, I prepared an elevation sketch of kitchen furniture, a diagram of the Ashgate Home and Farm, and a forensic diagram of the kitchen.

Custody of Evidence

At 1015 hours on September 8, YR-1, I received a call from Senior I.D. Technician Robin Mulligan that Mulligan had concluded the fingerprint examination and returned items #1–34 to Detective Lee. Approximately one-half hour later, I retrieved items #1–34. I began my examination at approximately 1400 hours on September 8, YR-1, and concluded my examination on September 10, YR-1, at 0930 hours.

Blood Examination

Item 2: Test results indicate the presence of blood in six stain areas on the knife. Side 1: A, B, C, and D. Side 2: E and F. Human deoxyribonucleic acid (DNA) was isolated from all six stains and tested. See conclusions for results. Item 2 was not swabbed for gunshot powder residue so as to not contaminate the blood found on the knife.

Item 9: Test results indicate the presence of blood in two stain areas on Sarah Baker's right shoe, designated 1 and 2. Stain area 1 is located on the upper-right side of the right shoe. Stain area 2 is located on the bottom of the right shoe, again at the upper-right side. Human DNA was isolated from both stains. See conclusions for results.

Item 11: No alcohol, morphine, cocaine, benzoylecgonine, cannabinoids, acidic or neutral drug, or other alkaline extractable drugs were detected. Human DNA was isolated from the blood sample of Sarah Baker for comparison testing.

Item 12: Test results indicate no presence of blood on the pants of Sarah Baker.

Item 13: Test results indicate no presence of blood on the blouse of Sarah Baker.

Items 14a and 14b: Test results indicated the presence of blood on the swab from the floor in front of the sink in the kitchen (14a) and where Kelly Baker's body was found (14b). Human DNA was isolated from these swabs. See conclusions for results.

Items 15 and 16: Test results indicated the presence of blood on the swabs from the blood spatter on the wall (15) and from the droplets on the chair (16) in the kitchen. Human DNA was isolated from these swabs. In an effort to determine whether Item 15 contained any saliva, I administered an amylase test on the blood swab. Amylase is an enzyme made by the salivary glands that helps the body break down carbohydrates. That test revealed no saliva present. The absence of saliva in the sample indicates that the spatter was not the result of forceful expectorating from the mouth.

Item 19: Test results indicated the presence of blood on the dish towel found on the kitchen counter by the sink. Human DNA was isolated from the stain. See conclusions for results.

Item 28: No morphine, cocaine, benzoylecgonine, cannabinoids, acidic or neutral drug, or other alkaline extractable drugs were detected. Alcohol was detected. Sample contained blood alcohol .08 percent by weight. Human DNA was isolated from the blood sample of Kelly Baker for comparison testing.

Item 29: Test results indicated the presence of blood in two stained areas, designated A and B, on the robe from Kelly Baker. Stain area A is located on the exterior left at the middle back level. Stain area B is located on the exterior right front chest. Human DNA was isolated from the stained areas designated A and B on the robe. See conclusions for results.

Item 30: Test results indicated the presence of blood in three stained areas, designated A, B, and C, on the pajamas from Kelly Baker. Stain area A is located on the exterior right rear of the pants below the waistband. Stain area B is located on the exterior right and left front of the pants just below the waist and extending down both thighs. Stain area C is located on the pajama top in the center back extending down to the bottom of the back of the pajama top. Human DNA was isolated from the stained areas designated A, B, and C on the pajamas. See conclusions for results.

Blood Conclusions

Based on the above analysis and testing:

- The DNA profile obtained from the stained swab from the floor in front of the sink in the kitchen (Item 14a), and the stain area on the dish towel (Item 19) is consistent with the DNA profile of Sarah Baker and different from the DNA profile of Kelly Baker. Therefore, Sarah Baker cannot be eliminated as a possible contributor to the genetic material isolated from these samples. Kelly Baker is eliminated as a possible contributor of this genetic material.

- The DNA profile obtained from the stain areas designated B, C, D, and F located on the knife found in Kelly Baker's hand (Item 2), the stain areas designated 1 and 2 on the shoes from Sarah Baker (Item 9), the stained swabs from the floor where Kelly Baker's body was found (Item 14b), the wall (Item 15), the kitchen chair (Item 16), the stain areas designated A and B on the robe from Kelly Baker (Item 29), and the stain areas designated A, B, and C from the pajamas from Kelly Baker (Item 30) is consistent with the DNA profile of Kelly Baker and different from the DNA profile of Sarah Baker. Therefore, Kelly Baker cannot be eliminated as a possible contributor of the genetic material isolated from these samples. Sarah Baker is eliminated as a possible contributor of this genetic material.

- The DNA profile obtained from the stain areas designated A and E on the knife (Item 2) are consistent with a mixture of the DNA profiles of Sarah Baker and Kelly Baker. Therefore, neither Sarah Baker nor Kelly Baker can be eliminated as possible co-contributors of this genetic material.

Blood Spatter and Pooling Measurements

Blood spatter on the wall measured at forty-two to forty-six inches from the floor.
Blood pooling around Mr. Baker's body measured six inches at the farthest point.

Firearms Examination

Examination of Item 1 pistol revealed it to be a World War II vintage 9mm Luger pistol, serial number 6851, in mechanical operating condition with the safety features functioning properly.

Examination of Item 8 revolver revealed it to be a Smith and Wesson .38-caliber double-action revolver, serial number F017052, in mechanical operating condition with the safety features functioning properly.

The Remington-Peters 9mm Luger cartridge cases, Items 3, 4, and 5, and the 9mm Luger jacketed bullets, Items 31–34, were identified as having been fired by the Item 1 pistol.

The Remington-Peters 9mm Luger cartridge, Item 6a, was identified as having been loaded into and extracted from the Item 1 pistol.

The Remington-Peters 9mm Luger cartridges, Item 24, are the types designed for use with a firearm such as the Item 1 pistol. The cartridges are the same type and brand as the Items 3, 4, and 5 cartridge cases, and Items 6a–d cartridges, and they are loaded with jacketed bullets similar to Items 31–34 bullets. When a jacketed bullet is fired from a semi-automatic pistol like a Luger, the gun automatically ejects the jacket as the bullet is fired from the gun. This accounts for empty cartridges (aka shell casings) being found on the floor.

Examination of Items 29 and 30, the robe and pajamas of Kelly Baker, reveal holes consistent with entrance bullet holes in the right shoulder and right upper chest. Additionally, there are three holes in the back; holes consistent with right-to-left grazing entrance and exit in the right back and a separate exit hole in the left back. Microscopic and chemical examination of the areas surrounding the bullet holes failed to reveal residues or muzzle-burn marks suitable for accurate muzzle-to-garment distance determinations. Further examination did not reveal any gunshot residues on Items 29 or 30.

Forensic Conclusions

I test-fired Item #1, the 9mm Luger pistol, shooting targets from a variety of distances. I found that gunpowder residue was left from a muzzle-to-target distance of four feet or less. Therefore, I concluded that the gun Sarah Baker fired must have been more than four feet from Kelly Baker's body at the time of firing.

Based on the location of Kelly Baker's blood spatter at forty-two to forty-six inches from the floor, the presence of a blood void on the kitchen chair and the lack of blood void on the victim's right palm (see below); the location of the two bullets recovered from the wall—one at thirty-one-inch height and the other at thirty-three-inch height; the downward trajectory of the two bullets recovered from the body of Kelly Baker; my use of a Styrofoam dummy to reconstruct the trajectory of the bullets; and the DNA analysis of the blood spatter and chair stains consistent with the blood of Kelly Baker leads me to conclude that Kelly Baker was seated when he was shot.

The circular bloodstains on the kitchen chair led me to conclude that Mr. Baker was seated when he was shot as there is a void (absence of blood) where his buttocks and legs would have been located. The blood droplets on the chair are consistent with blood dripping from Kelly Baker's body during and/or after being shot. The two blood spatter patterns on the wall are consistent with the two high-velocity gunshots that exited the body. High-velocity blood spatter occurs when the force of a bullet pushes blood out of the body at a high rate of speed in the direction the bullet is traveling as it exits the body. Of course, a body can bleed from an entry gunshot wound, as well. There was no blood spatter found on the kitchen table, indicating that Kelly Baker's body was not in front of the table at any point as he was being shot.

The presence of Kelly Baker's blood on the handle of the knife and the coroner's finding that there was blood on Kelly Baker's right palm leads me to conclude that the knife was placed in Kelly Baker's hand after he was shot and that it was not, as Sarah Baker claimed, in his hand when he allegedly attacked her. This is because if the knife was in his hand and the handle was pressed against his palm when he was shot, there would be a void (absence of blood) on his palm and the knife handle. Further, the presence of blood on the outer right side and bottom of Sarah Baker's right shoe indicates that she walked near the body while the blood was pooling to place the knife in Kelly Baker's right hand, explaining why some blood was on her right shoe (not her left), stepping backward as she retreated. Finally, the absence of high-velocity blood spatter on the knife's blade is inconsistent with Ms. Baker's claim of being attacked with the knife at the time of the shooting because I would expect to see blood spatter on the knife blade under such a factual scenario.

Release of Evidence to Detective Lee

On September 10, YR-1, at approximately 1135 hours at the Crime Laboratory, I turned over items #1–34 to Detective Lee for safekeeping.

I certify that I performed the above analyses and examinations as an employee of and in a laboratory operated by the Bureau of Forensic Science and that the above is an accurate record of the results of those analyses and examinations. I hold my conclusions to a reasonable degree of scientific certainty.

Dannie Rodriquez

Dannie Rodriguez
Forensic Scientist

Exhibit 22

Blood Spatter on East Wall in Kitchen

EXHIBIT 22-A

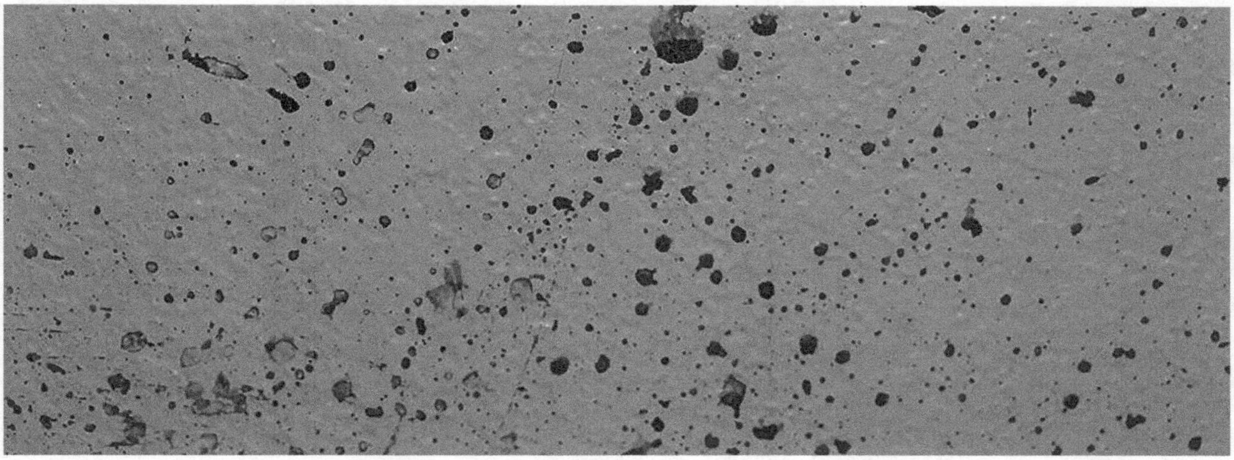

EXHIBIT 22-B

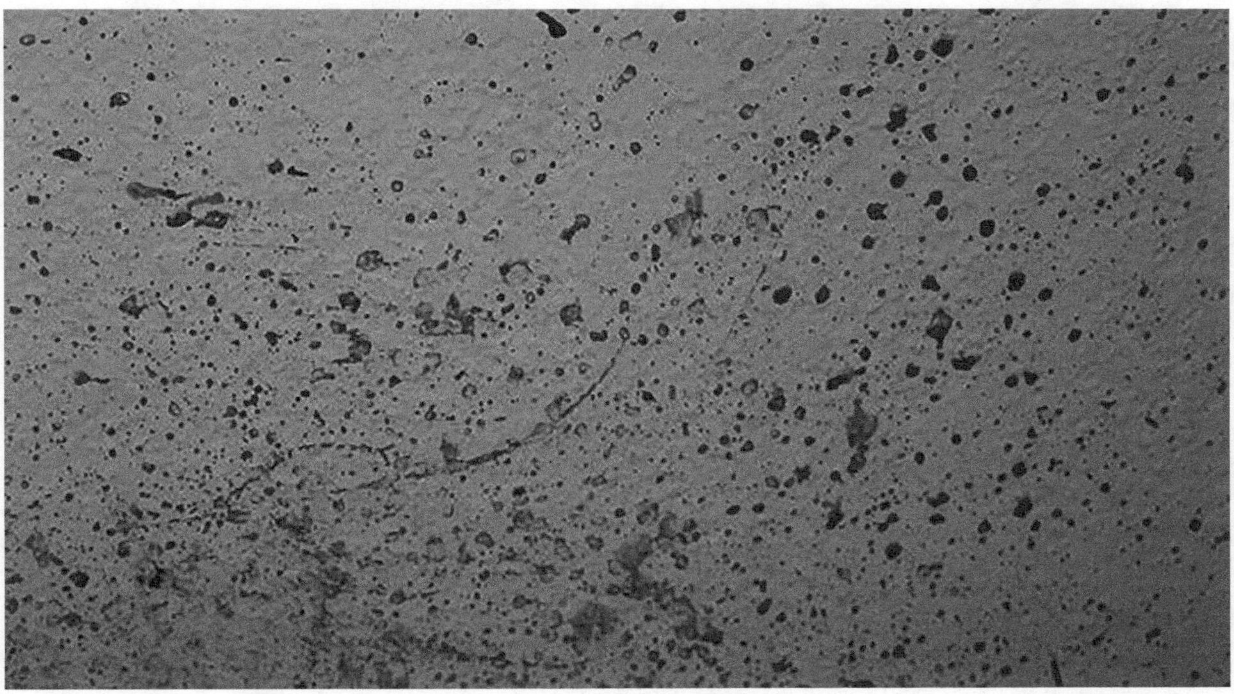

Exhibit 23

Blood Spatter on Kitchen Chair

Exhibit 24

Blood on Kitchen Floor

Exhibit 25

Blood Droplet in Front of Kitchen Sink

Exhibit 25

Blood Droplet in Front of Kitchen Sink

Exhibit 26

Kitchen Towel with Blood

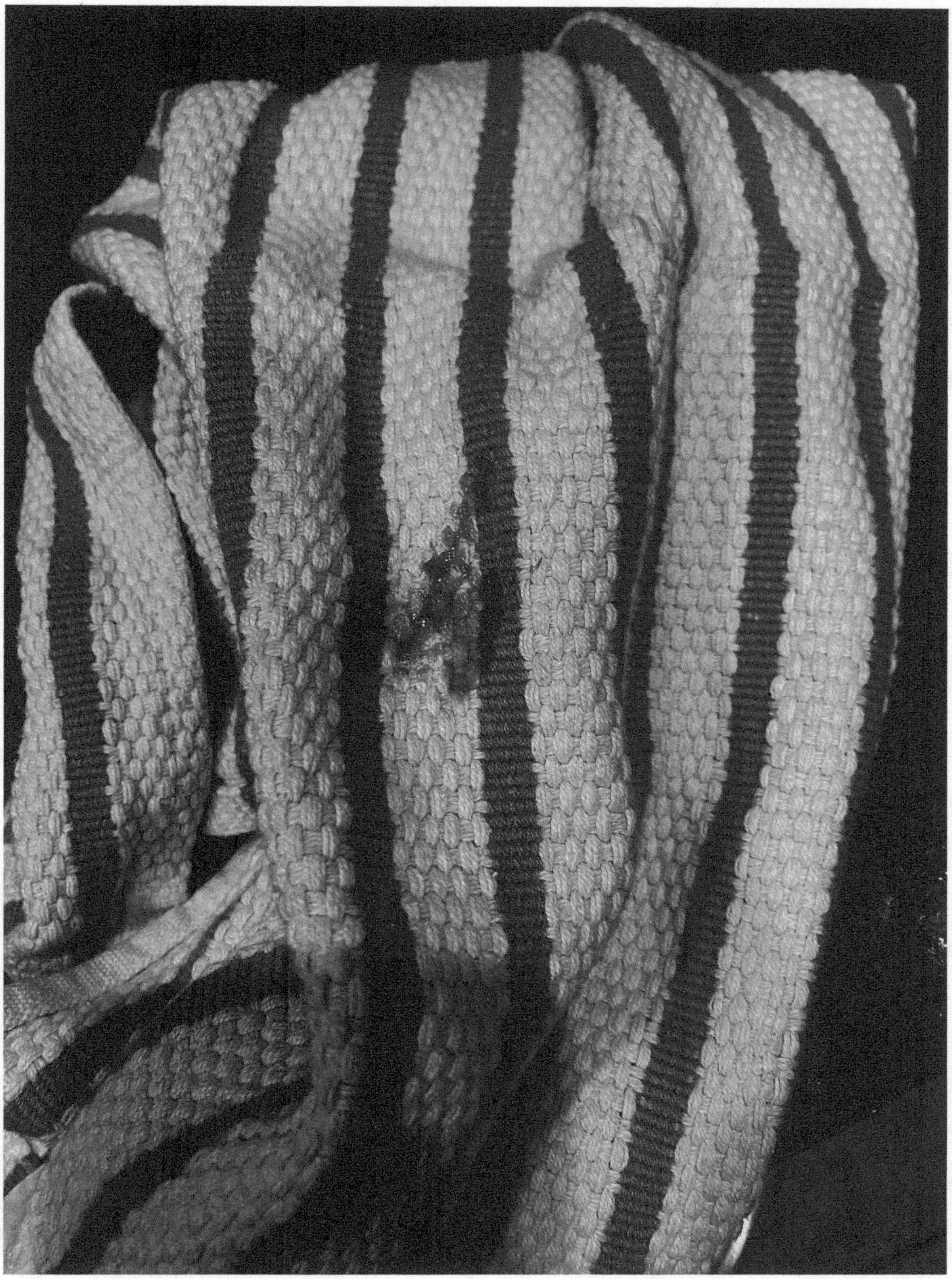

Exhibit 27

Sarah Baker's Shoes with Blood

27-A

27-B

Exhibit 27 (cont.)

27-C

27-D

27-E

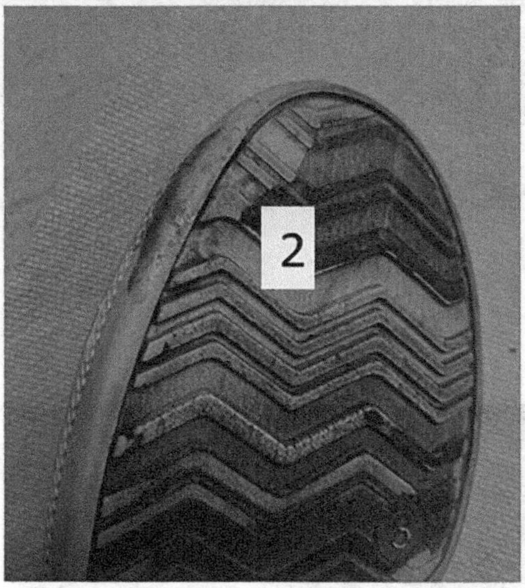

27-F

Résumé of Dannie Rodriguez
Forensic Scientist

EDUCATION

- B.S. Forensic Science with distinction, May YR-14, Nita State University. Minor in Chemistry.
- M.S. Forensic Science, June YR-12, Nita University.

EMPLOYMENT HISTORY

- Forensic Scientist III, Darrow County Sheriff's Department, April YR-5 to present.
- Forensic Scientist II, Darrow County Sheriff's Department, April YR-7 to April YR-5.
- Criminalist II, District Attorney's Laboratory of Criminalistics, Sheldon County, Nita, July YR-9 to April YR-7.
- Criminalist I, Arizona Department of Public Safety, Eastern Regional Crime Laboratory, Mesa, Arizona, September YR-13 to July YR-9.
- Fellowship, FBI Laboratory, Washington, D.C. Special studies in serology and DNA testing, June YR-12 to August YR-11.

PROFESSIONAL MEMBERSHIPS

- International Association of Blood Pattern Analysts since YR-3.
- International Association for Identification since YR-7.
- Nita Association of Crime Scene Investigators since YR-7.
- Association of Firearm and Toolmark Examiners since YR-8 (Distinguished Member status).
- American Academy of Forensic Sciences since YR-5.

CERTIFICATION

- Diplomate, American Board of Criminalistics, YR-4 to present.
- Nita Association of Forensic Scientists, YR-7 to present.

SPECIAL TRAINING

- Crime Scene Investigation and Reconstruction—Over 160 hours including specialized courses in Bloodstain Evidence, Gunshot Trajectory, and Blood Spatter Documentation.
- Firearms Related—More than 180 hours including specialized courses in Firearm and Toolmark Identification, Forensic Wound Pathology, and Wound Ballistics.
- Trace Evidence and Serology Related Over 250 hours including specialized training in DNA Analysis and Typing Methods, Hair/Fiber and Blood Collection and Analysis, Semen and Saliva Analysis, Human Population Genetics, Applied Molecular Spectroscopy, and Advanced Forensic Microscopy.

PROFESSIONAL PUBLICATIONS

- Preparation for a *Kelly* Admissibility Hearing in a RFLP DNA Case, *National Institute of Justice Review*, December YR-2.
- Shooting Reconstructions Utilizing Blood Spatter Patterns, *Nita Criminalistics Journal*, November YR-4.

- Reconstruction of Gunshot Homicide with Claim of Self-Defense, *American Forensic Science Quarterly*, October YR-7.
- Firearms Comparison with Remington Brand Caliber .22 Rimfire Bullets, *Police Science Journal*, February YR-9.

TEACHING EXPERIENCE

- Adjunct Professor at Nita State University, January YR-3 to present. Teach Biological Evidence Examination.
- Guest Lecturer at Nita State University, Nita University, Arizona State University, and the FBI Academy.
- Lectured on DNA Typing Methods, Crime Scene Investigation and Reconstruction, Gunshot Trajectory, and Firearms Examination and Identification.
- Staff and Guest Instructor for Law Enforcement Training Programs including courses presented by the Darrow County Sheriff's Department, the Nita City Police Department, the Nita State Investigators Association, and the Nita Crime Scene Investigators Association.

Exhibit 28

Darrow County Sheriff's Department
Office of Internal Affairs
Official Report

Incident Type/Offense	**Location**	**Reporting Officer**
CC 27543—Tampering with Physical Evidence	123 Norwalk Blvd Nita City, Nita	Avery Ozark Detective
Date/Time Reported	**Date/Time Occurred**	
February 18, YR-5		

Persons		
Role	Name	
Arrestee/Suspect	Robin Mulligan	

From January through February 15, YR-5 there had been a string of reported motor vehicle stops by an individual impersonating a police officer. The perpetrator, later identified as Jim Mulligan, son of Senior I.D. Technician of the Darrow County Sheriff's Department Robin Mulligan, had affixed his civilian car (a 1990 Crown Victoria) with a light rack on the roof, flashing headlights, and a siren. He would make unwarranted motor vehicle stops and yell at motorists for up to twenty minutes, including demanding they get out of the car to submit to sobriety tests, all while holding himself out to be an undercover member of the Darrow County Sheriff's Department. At the end of these encounters, Jim Mulligan would "let them off with a warning," but warn they "better not do it again" or else he would personally "hunt them down and hold them accountable for making Nita unsafe."

When complaints were made to the Darrow County Sheriff's Department about the behavior of this alleged officer, an investigation determined that this was a civilian impersonator and identified Jim Mulligan (DOB 12-20-YR-22) as the perpetrator. When officers from the Darrow County Sheriff's Department executed a search warrant at Mulligan's residence, the electronic equipment on the car had been removed and the car repainted. A subsequent internal investigation by the Office of Internal Affairs revealed that Senior I.D. Technician Robin Mulligan had learned of the investigation, tipped her son off that a search warrant was going to be executed, and helped him remove the lights and sirens from the car and repaint it prior to the execution of the search warrant. Although there was no evidence that Robin Mulligan was aware of, or in any way involved with, her son's impersonation of a police officer on multiple occasions, she did confess to destroying the evidence to help her son cover up his crimes because she "is first and foremost a mother and will do anything to protect her child."

Robin Mulligan was charged with tampering with physical evidence by the Darrow County District Attorney's Office, but she enrolled in a diversionary program and the charges were eventually dismissed. She was suspended for six months from the Sheriff's Department and demoted in rank. Although she was reinstated after the criminal charges were dismissed, there is a permanent record of this incident in her personnel file.

OFFICE OF THE DARROW COUNTY MEDICAL EXAMINER

354 Van Buren Avenue
Nita City, Nita
Report of Autopsy by County Medical Examiner

REPORT NO:	YR-1–1826	**DATE/TIME:**	09/08/YR-1 8:20 a.m.
DECEDENT	Kelly Lawrence Baker	**SEX:** Male	**AGE:** 42
HOME ADDRESS	8714 Springs Road Warrenton, Nita		
	Violent _X_ Casualty ___ Suicide___ Sudden when in apparent health___		
TYPE OF DEATH	Found dead ___ Suspicious, unusual, or unnatural _X_		
INVESTIGATING AGENCY	Nita County Sheriff's Office		
	Eyes: Brown	**Hair:** Brown, short	**Mustache/Beard:** NO
Description of Body	**Height:** 72"	**Weight:** 180 lbs	
	Rigor: Y	**Livor:** Reddish	**Distribution:** Posterior

Impressions:

See attached report

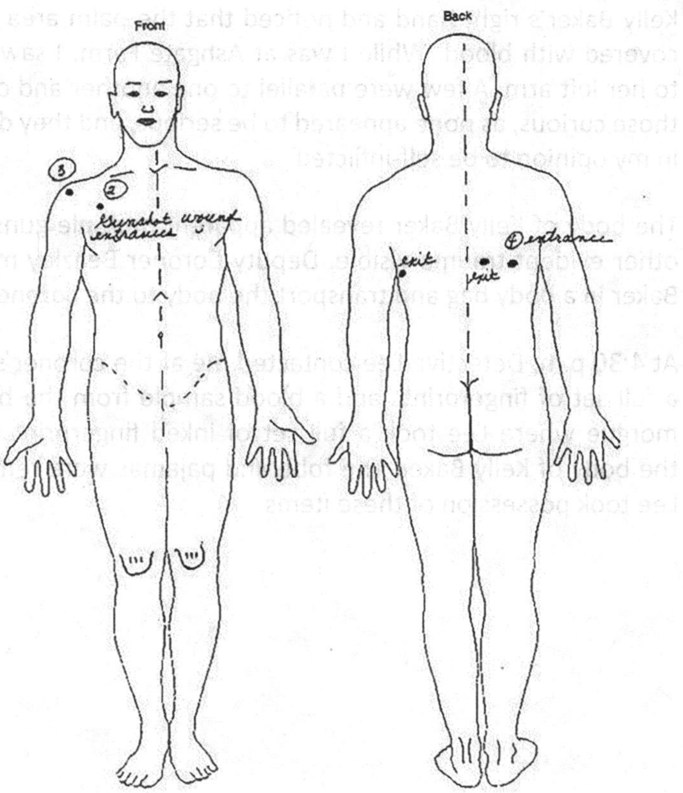

Probable Cause of Death	Manner of Death
Gunshot wounds of neck and thorax.	(check one only) Accident___ Natural___ Suicide___ Homicide _X_ Unknown___ Pending___
Date of autopsy: 09/08/YR-1	Location of Autopsy: Darrow Cty. Medical Examiner's Office 354 Van Buren Avenue, Nita City, Nita

Autopsy Record—Supplemental Report

Autopsy No.: 12–1826
Decedent: Kelly Lawrence Baker
Date: 09/08/YR-1

Initial Investigation

At 8:55 a.m. on September 7, YR-1, I received a call from Deputy Coroner Clem Beazley informing me that there had been a suspected homicide at Ashgate Farm in the county. Deputy Coroner Beazley met me at the coroner's office, and we drove to Ashgate Farm, arriving at 9:35 a.m. Detective Lee of the sheriff's department escorted us into the kitchen area. There I saw the body of an adult male identified to me as Kelly Baker, who was lying face down on the kitchen floor. There was blood on the floor and on Kelly Baker's face, chest, right arm, and back. His right hand and forearm were under his body. His body was still warm to the touch. Detective Lee informed me that there was a knife in Kelly Baker's right hand when Lee first arrived, but Lee took possession of the knife and placed it in an evidence bag. I examined Kelly Baker's right hand and noticed that the palm area and the anterior surfaces of the fingers were covered with blood. While I was at Ashgate Farm, I saw Sarah Baker. She had several superficial cuts to her left arm. A few were parallel to one another and clustered together on her left forearm. I found those curious, as none appeared to be serious, and they did not even require bandaging. They appeared in my opinion to be self-inflicted.

The body of Kelly Baker revealed apparent multiple gunshot wounds. There did not appear to be any other evident trauma visible. Deputy Coroner Beazley made arrangements to place the body of Kelly Baker in a body bag and transport the body to the coroner's office.

At 4:30 p.m. Detective Lee contacted me at the coroner's office and requested the opportunity to take a full set of fingerprints and a blood sample from the body of Kelly Baker. I accompanied Lee to the morgue where Lee took a full set of inked fingerprint impressions, and I took a vial of blood from the body of Kelly Baker. The robe and pajamas were removed from the body of Kelly Baker. Detective Lee took possession of these items.

Report of Autopsy

Pathological Diagnosis

1) **Penetrating gunshot wound with entrance on right side of face and injury to right carotid artery.**

2) **Perforating gunshot wound with entrance on right upper chest, injury to pulmonary artery trunk, heart and lungs, bilateral hemothoraces, and exit from lateral left thorax.**

3) Penetrating gunshot wound with entrance on the lateral right shoulder and injury to soft tissue and bone.

4) Perforating gunshot wound with entrance on right back, injury to soft tissue, and exit from right back.

General Description and External Examination

Rigor: Complete Livor: Reddish Distribution: Posterior

This is the body of a well-developed and nourished male. The body was in a body bag. Paper bags were over the hands. Fingerprint ink was on the fingertips. The body was unclothed. There were no personal effects. There was a 12-cm scar on the lower back. There were no tattoos. There was no external evidence of medical intervention. The external evidence of trauma consisted exclusively of gunshot wounds (see below). No other external evidence of trauma was found. The fingernails were short and intact.

Gunshot Wounds

1) Penetrating gunshot wound with entrance on right side of face at 8" below the top of the head and 3-3/4" to the right of the midline; 1/4 × 3/16" irregular round wound with 1/16" marginal abrasion ring; no evidence of powder debris. The wound track passes backward, downward, and leftward, perforating the right common carotid artery and soft tissue of the neck and back. A large caliber bullet with a deformed side was recovered in the subcutaneous tissue of back at 10" below the top of the head and 1-1/4" to the right of the posterior midline.

2) Perforating gunshot wound with entrance on right upper chest at 13" below the top of the head and 2-3/4" right of the midline; 3/16" round wound with a 1/16" marginal abrasion ring and singeing of the right lateral margin, 1/8". The wound track passes backward, downward, and leftward, perforating the right second intercostal space, the right upper and lower lung lobes, the pulmonary arteries trunk to the lateral left ventricle of the heart, the left upper and lower lung lobes and the left lateral six intercostal space to exit the lateral left back at 18" below the top of the head and 9" left of the posterior midline through a 3/8 × 1/4" oval wound.

3) Penetrating gunshot wound with entrance on the lateral right shoulder at 10" below the top of the head and 7-1/4" to the right of the anterior midline; 3/16" round wound with a 1/16" marginal abrasion ring; no evidence of powder debris. The wound track passes backward, downward, and leftward, perforating and fracturing the head of the humerus, perforating soft tissue

of the chest wall, and the body of cervical vertebra number five. The wound track continues perforating and fracturing the left clavicle and terminates in the left shoulder just anterior to the head of the left humerus, where a large caliber jacketed bullet with a deformed side was recovered at 12-1/2" below the top of the head and 7" to the left of the midline.

4) Perforating gunshot wound with entrance on right back at 18-1/2" below the top of the head and 4" right of the midline; 3/8 × 1/4" oval wound with lateral guttering, 1 × 3/8". The wound track passes downward, and leftward, perforating soft tissue of back to exit the right back at 18-5/8" below the top of the head and 2" to the right of the midline through a 1/2 × 3/8" oval wound with a medial guttering, 1-1/4 × 1/2".

Internal Examination

The body is opened with the usual Y-shaped incision. The organs of the thoracic and abdominal cavities are in their normal anatomic positions.

Pleura and Pericardium

Missile wound track; bilateral hemothoraces, partially clotted blood, approximately 75 ml right and 1000 ml left.

Peritoneum

Intact, smooth, and glistening.

Heart

350 gm. Right ventricle, three mm; left ventricle, thirteen mm. No valvular or congenital abnormalities. Coronary arteries, normal origin and distribution; right coronary artery predominant; left anterior descending, right coronary artery and left circumflex, no significant sclerosis all segments. Myocardium, missile wound track involving pulmonary artery trunk and left ventricle; no evidence of inflammation or fibrosis. Aorta, no significant alteration.

Lungs

Right 310 gm; left 230 gm. Hyoid bone, no evidence of trauma. Larynx, trachea, and bronchi intact and free of trauma or obstruction. Lungs, missile wound track of right upper and lower lobes and left upper and lower lobes; no evidence of inflammation or pulmonary artery emboli. Hemidiaphragms intact.

Liver

1405 gm. Capsule intact and smooth; parenchyma, no evidence of trauma, inflammation, or fibrosis.

Gallbladder

No significant alteration.

Spleen

65 gm. Capsule intact; parenchyma, no significant alteration.

Pancreas, Thyroid Gland, And Adrenal Glands

No significant alteration.

G.I. Tract

Esophagus, stomach, small and large intestine, no evidence of trauma, hemorrhage, or ulceration. Appendix present. Stomach contains approximately 120 ml of creamy, tan fluid with soft tan food fragments.

Kidneys

120 gm each. Capsules strip with ease revealing intact, smooth cortical surfaces; parenchyma, no evidence of trauma or inflammation.

Urinary Bladder

Wall intact, contains approximately 20 ml of clear yellow urine.

Genitalia

Prostate and testes, no significant alteration.

Head

The scalp is reflected following an intermastoid incision, and the calvarium is removed. Scalp and skull, no evidence of trauma. Cerebral meninges and brain, no evidence of trauma, hemorrhage, or inflammation; brain, 1370 gm. Cerebrospinal fluid, clear. Circle of Willis, no significant alteration.

Skeletal System

No evidence of trauma except along missile wound tracks.

Microscopics

Sections of skin taken from the entrance wounds labeled #1, #2, #3, and #4 are negative for powder debris. Sections of pulmonary artery, heart, and lung taken from along missile wound tracks reveal hemorrhage and tissue disruption. Sections of liver show no significant alteration.

Toxicology

The blood was screened by Forensic Scientist Dannie Rodriguez of the Crime Laboratory for morphine, cocaine, benzoylecgonine, cannabinoids, acidic or neutral drugs, or other alkaline extractable drugs. None was detected. The blood was also screened for alcohol and was determined to be .08 percent by weight. For more details including DNA analysis see the Crime Lab report by Dannie Rodriguez.

X-Rays

Six (6) X-Rays of the head, thorax, and abdomen show the bullets (2) in the neck and thorax.

Summary

The deceased was shot by an assailant.

Cause of Death

Gunshot wounds of neck and thorax.

Disposition of Evidence

Vial of blood to Detective Lee on 09-07-YR-1 at 4:30 p.m. Two bullets to Detective Lee on 09-08-YR-1 at 1:00 p.m. Body and clothing to Metropolitan for Triner Funeral Home on 09-09-YR-1 at 9:30 a.m.

Morgan P. Kahn

Morgan P. Kahn, MD
Medical Examiner and Forensic Pathologist
Darrow County
Nita City, Nita 99995
Dictated 09/10/YR-1
Signed 09/11/YR-1

Exhibit 29

Body Diagram—Kelly Baker

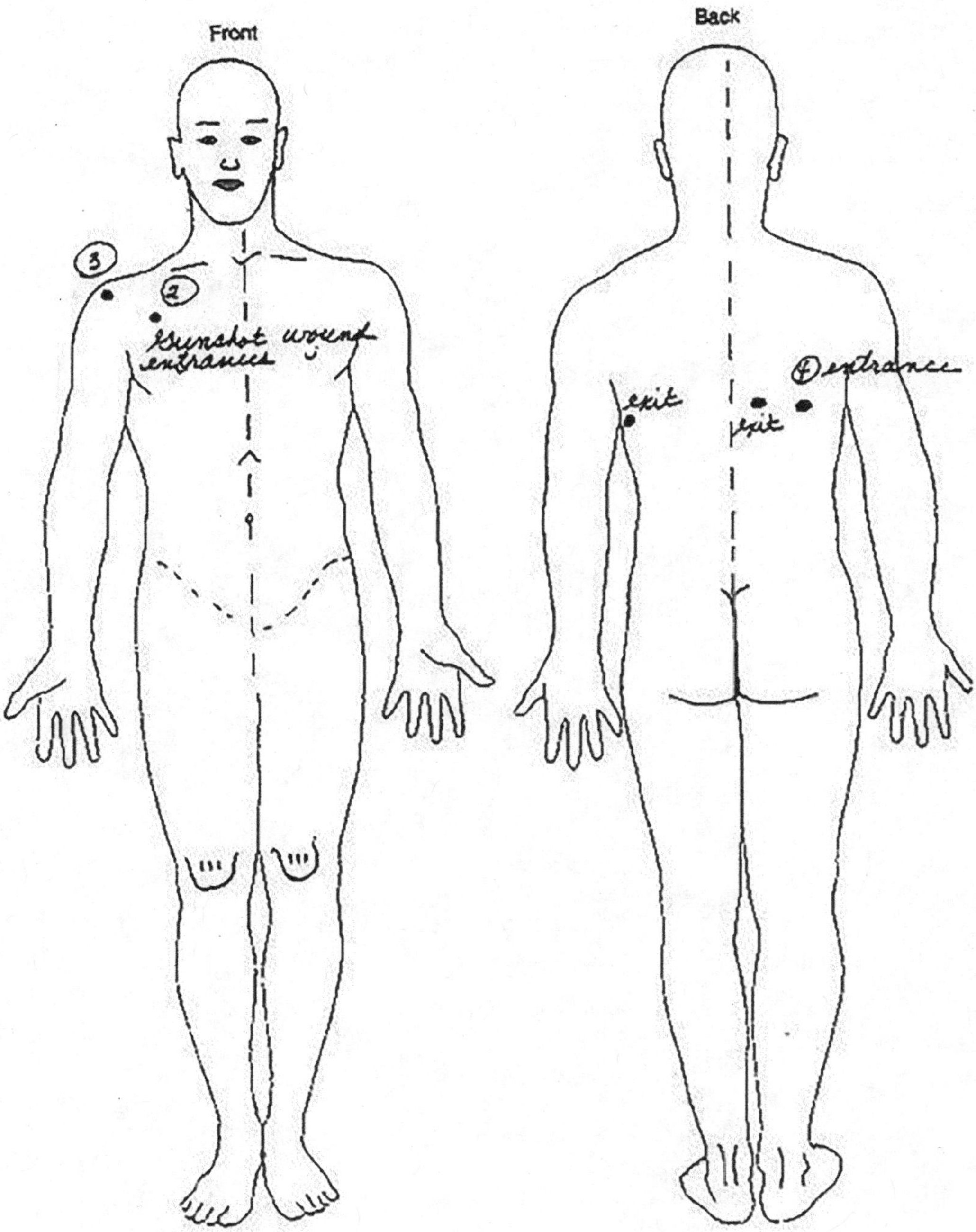

Decedent's Name: Kelly Lawrence Baker

Examined By: Morgan P. Kahn, MD   Date: 9/8/YR-1

Exhibit 30

Head Diagram—Kelly Baker

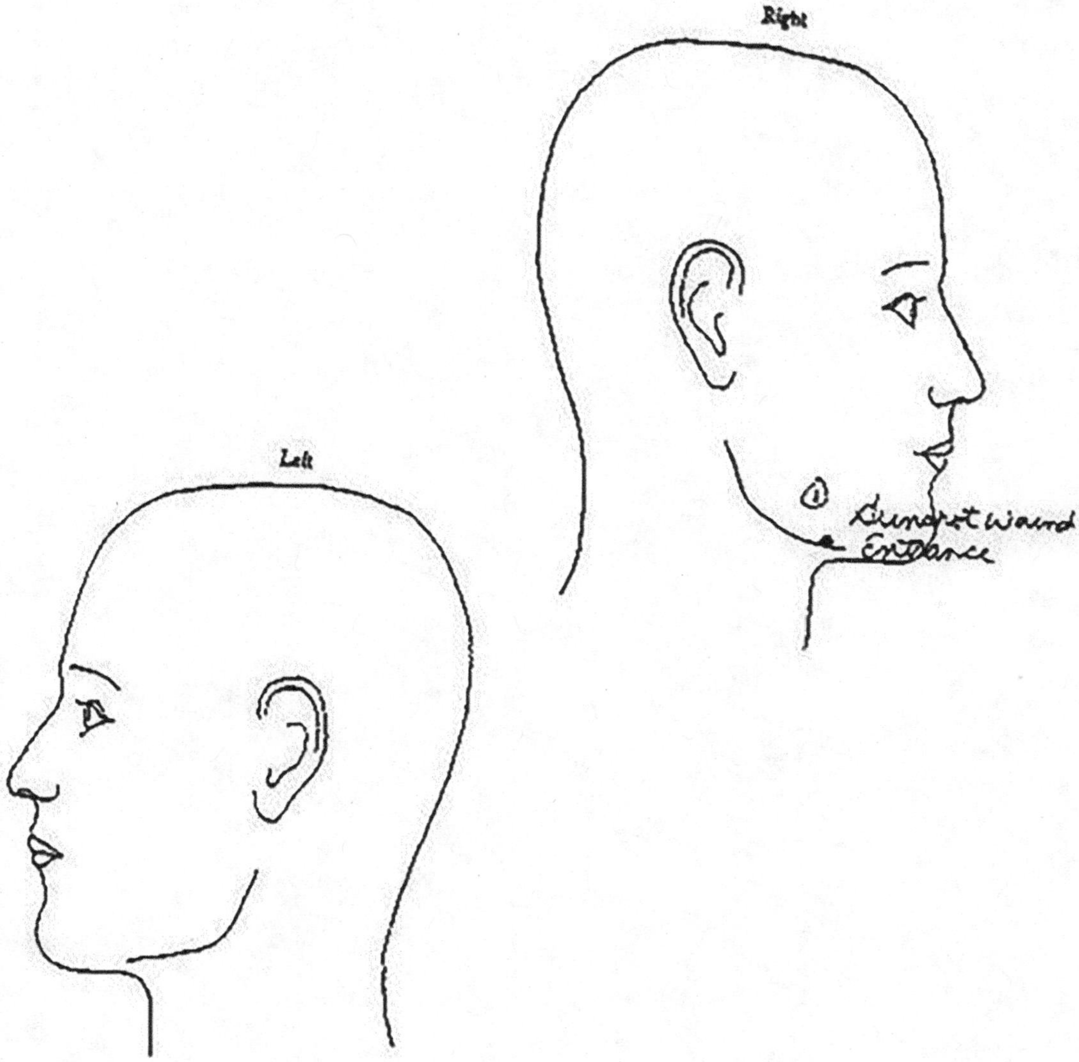

Decedent's Name: Kelly Lawrence Baker

Examined By: Morgan P. Kahn, MD   Date: 9/8/YR-1

Exhibit 31

Gunshot Wound Chart

			Wound No.							
			1		2		3		4	
			Ent	Bullet	Ent	Exit	Ent	Bullet	Ent	Exit
1. Location of Wound		Head								
		Neck	X							
		Chest			X					
		Abdomen								
		Back				X			X	X
	Arm	Right					X			
		Left								
	Leg	Right								
		Left								
2. Size of Wound		Diam.			3/16		3/16			
		Width	3/16			1/4			1/4	3/8
		Length	1/4			3/8			3/8	1/2
3. Inches from Wound to:		Top of head	8	10	13	18½	10	12½	18½	18-5/8
		Right of midline	3¾	1¼	2¾		7¼		4	2
		Left of midline				9		7		
4. Powder Debris		On skin								
		Clothing								
5. Direction of Bullet Through Body		Backward	X		X		X			
		Forward								
		Downward	X		X		X		X	
		Upward								
		To right								
		To left	X		X		X		X	
6. Bullet Found		Caliber	X		NO		X		NO	

Name: Kelly Lawrence Baker — City or County: Nita

Examined By: Morgan P. Kahn, MD — Date: 9/8/YR-1

Exhibit 32

Diagram of Sarah Baker's Left Arm Cuts

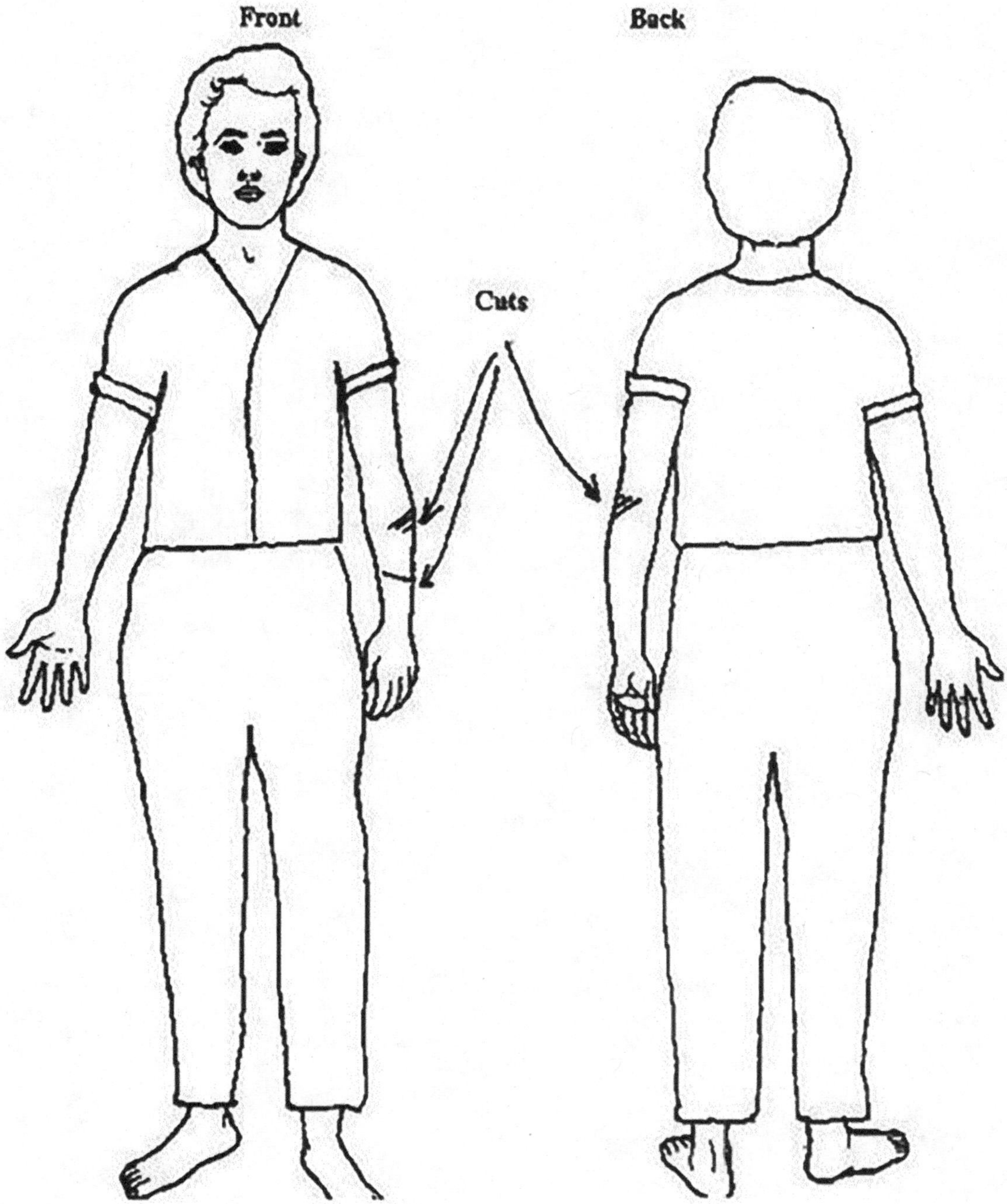

Examined By: Morgan P. Kahn, MD

Date: 9/7/YR-1

Arrest and Conviction Record of Sarah Hanna Baker

RE: WRIGHT, E. NAG DATE: 09-09-YR-1 TIME: 1630

CIR/C7184544

SEX/F

NAM/01 BAKER, SARAH HANNA

NAM/02 MARTIN, SARAH HANNA NDL/J2558782

SOC/696329331

****

ARR/DET/CITE/CONV:

#1

04-10-YR-2 CIT. DCSO CC 12031- UNLAWFUL DISCHARGE OF FIREARM

04-17-YR-2 CONVICTED, MISDEAMOR CC 12031-UNLAWFUL DISCHARGE OF FIREARM, FINE $500.

NOT TO BE DUPLICATED

Darrow County Sheriff's Department
Nita City, Nita
Offense Report #YR-2–04331
Report entered: 09/7/YR-1

Incident Type/Offense	Location	Reporting Officer
CC 12031—Discharge of Firearm in Unincorporated Area	Ashgate Farm 8714 Springs Road Warrenton, Nita	Deputy Marian Bracken Badge Number 344
Date/Time Reported	**Date/Time Occurred**	
04/10/YR-2, 19:53		

Persons		
Role	**Name**	
Victim	William H. White	
Arrestee/Suspect	Sarah Baker	

DCSD Offense Report
CC 12031—Unlawful Discharge of Firearm

Narrative

At 1935 hours I was patrolling the east Warrenton area when I received a call from dispatch of a shooting at Ashgate Farm. I responded to the Shell station at Springs Rd. and Gulliver Blvd., and at 1942 I spoke with the victim. He said that he had gone to Ashgate to discuss having purchased a pony from the farm that died a short time later. When he arrived at the farm, he spoke with someone named Kit. He gave up talking to Kit as Kit appeared to be intoxicated by alcohol, so he went to the main house and knocked on the door. Sarah Baker, the owner of Ashgate, answered the door. She refused to talk to him and ordered him off the property. She left, came back with a gun, and said she would kill him. He ran to his car. As he got about 100 feet away he heard shots but doesn't know where the shots went. He demanded that Ms. Baker be arrested for assault with a deadly weapon.

At 2015 hours I arrived at Ashgate Farm and spoke with Sarah Baker. She was agitated, at times crying, and claimed that the victim had come to her home, began yelling in front of her home, and when she went out, he threatened her. She ran to get a gun to protect herself. I asked her to explain the threat, and the victim said, "If you don't give me the money you owe me, I'll burn your house down with you in it." After she got the gun, the victim started to leave, turned around and said something, and she thought he was going to come back and hurt her. She fired the gun in the air twice, and he then turned and ran off. She said the only reason she used the gun was she had no other protection. The only other person nearby was an employee named Kit Manville, who takes care of the horses. She called Manville, but said Manville was obviously drunk again and wouldn't come to her aid. I checked the weapon, a 9mm Luger, serial #6851, and found four live rounds in the magazine and one in the chamber. I found three expended 9mm casings, two on the porch and one at the foot of the porch steps. I contacted Kit Manville, who appeared to be UI alcohol. Manville heard the shots but claimed not to have heard any of the conversation. I issued a citation to Sarah Baker for a violation of CC 12031, as it is illegal to fire a weapon in that area of the county unless in self-defense. I did not confiscate the weapon as Ms. Baker admitted firing the same.

ARREST AND CONVICTION RECORD OF KELLY LAWRENCE BAKER

RE: WRIGHT, E. NAG DATE: 09-14-YR-1 TIME: 1505
CIR/D4973134
NAM/01 BAKER, KELLY LAWRENCE NDL/J3559791
SOC/893314496

****

ARR/DET/CITE/CONV:

#1

05-03-YR-6 CIT. NCPD CC 242-BATTERY, MISDEMEANOR
05-24-YR-6 PLED NO CONTEST TO MISDEMEANOR DISTURBING THE PEACE, 6 MONTHS SUMMARY PROBATION, $200 FINE

****

#2

07-13-YR-6 ARREST NCPD CC 23152-DUI, MISDEMEANOR
08-08-YR-6 PLED GUILTY TO MISDEMEANOR DUI, 3 YEARS PROBATION, 2 DAYS COUNTY JAIL, $750 FINE

NOT TO BE DUPLICATED

Nita City Police Department
Nita City, Nita

Offense Report #YR-6–12117

Report entered: 05/3/YR-6

Incident Type/Offense	Location	Reporting Officer
CC 242—Battery	Cooney's Irish Pub 29 Plaza Walk Nita City, Nita	Officer Marni Culler Badge Number 88
Date/Time Reported	**Date/Time Occurred**	
05/03/YR-6, 22:45		

Persons		
Role	Name	
Victim	Sally Kehale	
Arrestee/Suspect	Kelly Baker	

DCSD Offense Report
CC 242—Battery with a Dangerous Instrument

Narrative

At 2245 hours I was patrolling the Plaza Walk area when I heard yelling coming from Cooney's Pub. I ran inside the bar and saw a man and a woman standing near the bar. The man was swearing and the woman was crying. I separated the two and could see that the man appeared to be under the influence of alcohol. I directed the man to sit at a table and then talked to the woman. The woman gave me her name as Sally Kehale.

Kehale said she was the cocktail waitress. She had mistakenly removed a glass from the man's table, and he became irate. When he discovered his glass was gone, he walked over to her, grabbed her by the arm, and yelled at her, "Where the hell is my drink?" She told him the drink was empty, and he shoved her against the wall yelling, "Don't you pull that stuff on me." She said that I arrived immediately after that happened. The bartender, Sheldon Fetzer, confirmed Ms. Kehale's account.

I then returned to the man involved in the incident. He gave me his name as Kelly Baker and told me that he worked for KNTA-TV. He said that he had joined KNTA about one year ago and was on the news team. He asked that I drop the matter, as it wouldn't be a very popular thing for the Nita Police to arrest a television personality. I told Mr. Baker that I would be happy to listen to his side of the story, but that witnesses had already confirmed that he had used profanities and roughly handled Ms. Kehale. Baker said that this bar was obviously "a dive," and they made their money by using tactics like removing their drinks before they were finished. I told Baker that he had a choice. Either he could leave the bar, in which case I would issue him a citation, or he could refuse, and I would arrest him and take him to jail. He said he would take the citation and leave. Ms. Kehale and Mr. Fetzer said they would appear as witnesses if necessary, and they could be reached at Cooney's. I issued the citation.

Nita City Police Department

Nita City, Nita

Offense Report #YR-5–17434

Report entered: 07/13/YR-5

Incident Type/Offense	Location	Reporting Officer
CC 23152—DUI		Officer Melinda Rowell Badge Number 167
Date/Time Reported	**Date/Time Occurred**	
07/13/YR-6, 01:45		

Persons		
Role	**Name**	
Victim		
Offendee/Suspect	Kelly Baker	

DCSD Offense Report

CC 23152—Misdemeanor Driving Under the Influence—Alcohol or Drugs

Narrative

At 0145 hours I was working swing DUI shift in a marked DUI vehicle proceeding eastbound on Rosecrans Blvd. west of Fulton St. I saw a Mercedes convertible southbound on Fulton turn left to go westbound on Rosecrans. The Mercedes screeched the tires making the turn, passed me, and proceeded westbound straddling the dividing line between the two Rosecrans westbound lanes. I made a U-turn at Fulton and followed the Mercedes for about six blocks. The Mercedes came to a stop at the intersection of Moore St. even though there was no signal or stop sign at that intersection and no vehicles crossing the intersection. I activated the overhead warning lights and followed. When the Mercedes did not stop, I activated the siren. The Mercedes slowly pulled over to the curb, parking the right front wheel slightly over the curb.

I approached the driver, who was alone, and asked him for identification. He had difficulty getting his wallet and then produced a Nita driver's license #J3559791 in the name of Kelly Baker. I recognized Mr. Baker from his television news appearances. I asked him where he was going, and he said home. I asked him where he was coming from, and he said there had been a little staff celebration because he was going to become a news anchor. Mr. Baker's speech was slurred, he smelled of some alcoholic beverage, and I told him that I was going to have to ask him to perform some sobriety tests. He pleaded with me, asking that I just take him home and forget the matter. I told him I could not do that. He said that he didn't want to "take any stupid goddamn tests" and said I had better let him go or my "job was on the line." I told him that he could either take the tests or I would have to take him downtown and arrest him. I then demonstrated the heel-to-toe test and asked him to take it. Mr. Baker took two or three steps and then fell to the side and said he didn't want to take any more tests. I then placed Mr. Baker under arrest, handcuffed him, and placed him in the back of my patrol car. I secured his YR-8 Mercedes-Benz SL500 roadster convertible and called a tow truck to take it to the impound lot. I then transported Mr. Baker to the Darrow County Jail. I informed Mr. Baker of his rights to a blood, breath, or urine test. Mr. Baker agreed to take a breath test. The breath test was administered in the prescribed manner, and Mr. Baker blew a .17 and a .18. He was then booked in the county jail.

ARREST AND CONVICTION RECORD OF KIT MANVILLE

RE: WRIGHT, E. NAG DATE: 09-11-YR-1 TIME: 1458

CIR/B7653449

NAM/01 MANVILLE, KIT

NDL/N7024377

SOC/535667984

****

ARR/DET/CITE/CONV:

#1

11-10-YR-13 ARREST NCPD CC 23152-DUI, MISDEMEANOR

11-22-YR-13 CONVICTED, PLEA OF GUILTY, MISDEMEANOR DUI: SEN. 2 YEARS FORMAL PROBATION, 2 DAYS COUNTY JAIL, FINE $750

04-27-YR-12 VIOLATION OF PROBATION, REVOKED & REINSTATED, 15 DAYS COUNTY JAIL

****

#2

04-03-YR-11 ARREST NHP CC 23152-DUI, MISDEMEANOR

04-27-YR-11 CONVICTED, PLEA OF GUILTY, MISDEMEANOR DUI W/PRIOR: SEN. 3 YEARS FORMAL PROBATION, 120 DAYS COUNTY JAIL CONCURRENT, FINE $1,500

01-17-YR-10 VIOLATION OF PROBATION, REVOKED, 90 DAYS COUNTY JAIL CONCURRENT

****

#3

12-02-YR-9 ARREST NHP CC 23152-DUI, MISDEMEANOR

12-08-YR-9 PART B INFORMATION FILED: MISDEMEANOR ENHANCED TO FELONY BASED ON TWO PRIOR DUI CONVICTIONS IN THE LAST 5 YEARS

01-17-YR-8 CONVICTED, JURY TRIAL, FELONY DUI W/2 PRIORS: SEN. 3 YEARS FORMAL PROBATION, 1 YEAR PRISON, $2,000 FINE

****

#4

09-02-YR-4 ARREST DCSD CC 537c-FRAUDULENT ANIMAL LOAN, MISDEMEANOR

09-09-YR-4 CONVICTED, PLEA OF GUILTY, CC 537c, 5 DAYS COUNTY JAIL, SUSPENDED, 1 YEAR FORMAL PROBATION, FINE $100, RESTITUTION

****

Arrest and Conviction Record of Chris Spanalski

RE: WRIGHT, E. NAG DATE: 09-16- YR-1 TIME: 1505

CIR/B9428731

NAM/01 SPANALSKI, CHRIS

NDL/F7882929

SOC/551422876

****

ARR/DET/CITE/CONV:

#1

03-13-YR-16 ARREST NSPD CC 484–EMBEZZLEMENT, FELONY

03-15-YR-16 RELEASED FROM CUSTODY, CHARGES DISMISSED, VICTIM REFUSED TO PROSECUTE

****

#2

1-25-YR-9 ARREST NSPD CC 520–ATTEMPTED BATTERY WITH A DANGEROUS INSTRUMENT, FELONY

3-14-YR-9 CONVICTED, PLEA OF GUILTY, 2 YEARS PROBATION, FINE $1,500

****

#3

10-25-YR-7 ARREST NSPD NITA EMPLOYMENT CODE(NEC) §1320-DIVERSION OF EMPLOYMENT BENEFITS, EMBELLEZMENT. MISDEMEANOR.

11-14-YR-7 SUBSTITUTE INFORMATION FILED AFTER RESTITUTION PAID. CHARGED OFFENSE REDUCED TO MISDEMEANOR EMBEZZLEMENT. CONVICTION, PLEA OF GUILTY TO MISDEMEANOR EMBEZZLEMENT, 2 YEARS PROBATION.

****

NOT TO BE DUPLICATED

Testimony of Detective Casey Lee at Preliminary Hearing

Oath Administered

Direct Examination

My name is Casey Lee. I am a detective with the Darrow County Sheriff's Department. I have been employed by the department for eleven years. I started in patrol for five years, then spent one year in internal affairs, and have spent the last five years in the detective division. During those years I have worked on a variety of cases including homicides, robberies, burglaries, assaults, and batteries.

On September 7 of last year, I was working the day shift. At 8:52 a.m. I was at the station preparing a report when I got a call on my mobile radio from the dispatcher, Edel Karl, to respond to a homicide at Ashgate Farm just outside Warrenton. Karl informed me that Deputy Camelli was in the area and would secure the scene. I left immediately and arrived about eighteen minutes later. Deputy Camelli was already at the scene, and I took over handling the case.

When I arrived, Deputy Camelli was standing outside the home with the defendant and with the Ashgate manager, Chris Spanalski. Deputy Camelli told me that she had fully secured the residence, checking to make sure no one else was in the house. She found the body of the defendant's husband, Kelly Baker, lying face down in the kitchen. She said that she checked for vital signs and found none. She called the coroner's office, as the defendant had told her the shooting had taken place more than forty-five minutes earlier.

I entered the home and found that Deputy Camelli's observations were correct. I saw Kelly Baker's body lying face down. There was blood on the floor. He was holding a butcher knife in his right hand that was partially under his body. There was a 9mm Luger pistol in the kitchen along with four empty 9mm cartridges lying on the floor near the refrigerator. I took custody of the knife, the pistol, serial number 6851, with a live round in the chamber and three in the magazine, and the empty cartridges and placed them in separate evidence bags.

I then walked back outside to the front porch where the defendant was being detained by Deputy Camelli. I noticed that she appeared unusually calm, although she was talking to Deputy Camelli about her arm wounds. I looked at her left arm and noticed what appeared to be several minor cuts or scratches with a slight amount of blood. I noticed that she had blood on the side of her right shoe.

I contacted dispatch by radio and asked Karl to play the 911 recording for me. Based on the recording and my observations at the scene, I placed the defendant under arrest for the murder of her husband. The defendant asked if she could change her shoes. I told her to remove her shoes there and I placed them in an evidence bag. I then escorted her upstairs to her bedroom where she put on new pair of shoes.

The coroner's office personnel arrived and took custody of Kelly Baker's body. I asked Deputy Camelli to secure the scene and remain there until I returned with a search warrant and crime scene technician. I then transported the defendant to the Darrow County Jail for booking. While there I asked the medical staff to examine the defendant to see what her medical condition was. Nurse Alex Kouri, in my presence, examined the defendant's left arm and cleaned the cuts. The cuts did not require any further medical attention, such as stiches or staples. Nurse Kouri, at my direction and with the defendant's consent, obtained both blood and hair samples from the defendant and gave them to me in separate vials. Nurse Kouri then took the defendant behind a screened area, gave the defendant a prison uniform, and handed me the defendant's blouse and pants. I placed them in separate evidence bags.

Throughout the time the defendant was in my custody, including the time later when I took a full statement from her, she at no time displayed any emotion other than expressing a concern over her wounds to her left arm. She at no time expressed any remorse for her husband's death. All she seemed concerned about was when she was going to be bailed out.

We obtained a search warrant to search the Ashgate residence and Sarah Baker's cell phone. I executed the warrant for the residence with Darrow County Forensic Investigator Dannie Rodriguez at approximately 1:45 p.m. on September 7th. During the search of the second-story bedroom, I located a .38-caliber Smith and Wesson revolver that was fully loaded with six rounds. It was on a shelf in a closet. Immediately next to it was a closed box of .38-caliber ammunition containing ninety-four of the original 100 rounds. Next to that box was a closed box of 9mm Luger ammunition containing eighty-six of the original 100 rounds. I placed the revolver and the two ammunition boxes in separate evidence bags, which I retained. The clothing in the closet was all women's clothing.

Because the warrant authorized seizing relevant documents, I searched a desk in the same bedroom and found a document entitled, "Last Will and Testament of Sarah Baker," among other personal effects belonging to Sarah Baker, such as her Social Security card, birth certificate, and passport. I seized the will as evidence.

On the second floor south wing, I searched a bedroom containing personal effects of Kelly Baker, including his wallet and driver's license. There was no blood, no weapons, and no ammunition in the room. There was an empty bottle of whiskey and a glass on a night table that appeared to have traces of whiskey. On the bed we found an electronic tablet. I photographed it. Because the search warrant authorized us to search electronics, I touched the screen and the tablet "woke up." I did not need to enter a passcode. I looked in the "Notes" application and took a picture of a note from September 6th. I then looked at the search history on the tablet and saw that the last internet search made was, "How did OJ Simpson get caught?" I photographed the search history and seized the tablet as evidence.

Dannie Rodriguez accompanied me throughout the search. When we returned to the first floor, Rodriguez took measurements of the kitchen area and took samples of blood from the floor, the chair, and the wall. I pointed out to Rodriguez a plate and a coffee mug on the table, then took custody of those items for fingerprint testing.

The entire search of the premises took about two hours. We then drove to the residence occupied by Chris Spanalski, who is the farm manager. We were there approximately twenty minutes, and sometime around 4:15 p.m., I returned to the police department and searched Sarah Baker's cell phone in accordance with the warrant. What we found of significance during that search were text messages between Ms. Baker and Kendall Johnson, her and Kelly Baker, an email from Kendall Johnson, and her September call history.

I retained all the items of physical evidence I had secured in the search of the residence until September 8 when I turned certain items over to Senior I.D. Technician Mulligan and later Forensic Scientist Rodriguez. On September 10, Rodriguez returned all items to me. I have retained them for safekeeping since that date.

CROSS-EXAMINATION

The defendant was cooperative at all times from the time that I first encountered her outside Ashgate until I concluded my initial interview of her at the jail. She did not refuse to talk to me either at the scene or during the initial jail interview. When I advised her of her *Miranda* rights, she said that she understood she didn't have to talk to me, but she said she wanted me to know what happened. When I asked her if we could search her home, she refused, assuming we would plant evidence to support what she claimed was a bogus murder charge.

I did not contact any other people who worked for Ashgate Farm to see if anyone else witnessed the defendant and Kendall Johnson when they were on the property. I did not check to see if any maids, cooks, or groundskeepers were on the property the day that Kit Manville claimed to have seen them enter the house. I did not talk to anyone else who might have been present at The Saddle restaurant where the two had dinner. I did not conduct interviews of others who were present for meetings of the Battered Women Council or Project WEB as to how the two conducted themselves when they were both at those meetings. I did not contact fellow workers or former employers of Kit Manville to see what they would say about Manville's character for truth and honesty or Manville's feelings toward the defendant.

I did not search some of the other rooms to see if there were firearms or ammunition located elsewhere in the house. I did not see any blood in any of the locations I walked through or entered while searching the house. The only blood we located was in the kitchen. I did check our department records to see what firearm was used by the defendant in the April 10, YR-2, incident, and it was the 9mm Luger, serial #6851.

I did not check with Kelly Baker's friends, people he worked with, or former employers to determine what his character for violence was. I did locate two Nita Police Department reports that revealed a battery and a DUI conviction, but I did not check to see whether police records in areas where he had previously lived and worked showed any arrests or convictions. I understand that he previously worked for a TV station in Nevada. I believe it was in Las Vegas. I do know from working cases both as a detective and as a patrol officer that some people who are ordinarily law abiding and peaceful can become combative and assaultive when they are drinking.

I did not check Kelly Baker's hands when I found him on the floor. I only removed the knife for safety purposes. As I understand it, the only people who touched the body after Deputy Camelli arrived were Deputy Coroner Clem Beazley and Dr. Kahn. I have no personal knowledge whether there was or was not blood on the palm of Mr. Baker's right hand. I did not photograph the locations of the gun and the casings before I collected them. I did not measure the exact location of the gun and the casings before collecting them. I cannot say with 100 percent certainty that I placed the evidence placards exactly where the gun and casings were found, but I was very close. I saw Dannie Rodriguez use the evidence placards I placed when taking forensic measurements in the kitchen. I did not photograph, measure, or mark exactly where the knife was in relation to Mr. Baker's body, but it was in his right hand, partially under his body. I have seen Exhibit 6 and it fairly and accurately represents what I saw in the Baker's kitchen on September 7, YR-1.

I did find an empty bottle of whiskey and a glass on the night table in Mr. Baker's bedroom. There was a small amount of liquid in the glass, and it smelled like whiskey. I am aware that Mr. Baker's toxicology study showed that he had a blood alcohol level of .08 percent, but I can't give an opinion about how high it may have gotten during the night or whether he was impaired at the time of the incident.

I am aware that sometimes people who have to fight to defend themselves go into a shock-like state afterward and don't show any emotion for some time. I have seen that once or twice. I have also seen relatives of people who were killed delay their reactions because of shock. But I can tell you that I haven't seen anyone accused of killing someone who was any calmer than the defendant was that morning. I understand her friend Chris Spanalski says she was hysterical when Spanalski arrived, but all I can speak to is her demeanor as I observed it and she was calm and collected.

It is true that the defendant had what looked like cuts on her left arm, and there did appear to be a small amount of blood several places on her upper and lower left arm.

I have reviewed the foregoing and it is a true and correct transcription of my testimony on October 20, YR-1, at the preliminary hearing in State v. Baker, in the Darrow County District Court, Nita City, Nita.

Casey Lee

Detective Casey Lee, DCSD

Testimony of Dr. Morgan Kahn at Preliminary Hearing

Oath Administered

Direct Examination

I hold a medical degree (MD) and am a pathologist and director of the pathology laboratory of the Darrow County Coroner's Office here in Nita City. I have been a pathologist with that office since YR-8. I graduated from Tufts University with a BS in biology in YR-23. I received an MS in biology at Southern Methodist University in YR-11. In YR-15 I earned a PhD in experimental pathology and an MD at Case Western Reserve University. I was a resident in anatomic and clinical pathology at Duke University Medical Center from YR-15 through YR-12. I then served as an assistant chief medical examiner in Chapel Hill, North Carolina, for one year as part of a forensic pathology fellowship. I then became a forensic pathologist with the Diagnostic Pathology Medical Group in Nita City. In YR-8 I accepted a position as assistant director of pathology at the Darrow County Coroner's Office. Five years later I was appointed as the director. I have taught pathology at Nita University Medical School from YR-10 through YR-5. I am board certified in three fields of pathology: anatomical, clinical, and forensic. I also sit regularly on the certification board of the American Board of Pathology as an examiner of applicants for board certification.

A forensic pathologist is a medical doctor who investigates unexpected, suspicious, unnatural, and violent deaths. We do this by performing autopsies (a complete external and internal medical examination of a body after death). As a forensic pathologist, my job is to determine cause of death and manner of death. "Cause of death" is the underlying medical condition, disease, or injury that begins a lethal chain of events resulting in death. "Manner of death" is the way in which a death occurs, which may be classified in one of five ways: homicide (death caused by another person); suicide (self-inflicted death); accident (ex: car accident); natural causes (ex: cancer); or undetermined (when a specific manner cannot be deciphered). I collect, test, and interpret evidence found outside and inside a body to determine cause and manner of death. It is common for forensic pathologists to speak with police investigators and review crime scene evidence that relates to the death. I have testified in state and federal trial courts in this state and in North Carolina and given expert testimony in the field of forensic pathology on approximately 130 occasions. On most such occasions I was called by the prosecution, but in at least fifteen or sixteen cases I was called to testify as a defense witness. As a member of the medical staff of the coroner's office I am employed by Darrow County. I am also a member of the Nita Clinical Laboratory and am assistant chief of the Department of Pathology at Salk Hospital, both private institutions.

In the course of my work in North Carolina, Diagnostic Pathology Medical Group, and the Darrow County Coroner's Office, I have performed approximately 3,000 autopsies, around 25 percent of which were classified as gunshot deaths. I qualified as an expert and testified in court and rendered opinions with respect to gunshot death cases on more than thirty occasions. I have lectured in the field of gunshot wound deaths before groups of doctors, police officers, and medical staffs of hospitals and have taken part in professional group discussions in this area.

On September 7, YR-1, I was at the Darrow County Coroner's Office when Deputy Coroner Beazley received a call that there had been a shooting at Ashgate Farm, just outside of Warrenton. The two of us drove to Ashgate, arriving there sometime around 9:30 a.m. I was escorted inside the house to the kitchen area. There I saw the body of Kelly Baker. It was obvious that Mr. Baker had been dead for at least an hour, but no more than two hours because rigor mortis—the stiffening of the body about two hours after death—had not yet set in. Mr. Baker was lying face down on the floor. I checked and found no pulse. His body was still slightly warm, and there was blood on his face, his right arm—which was partially under his torso—and on the floor. Mr. Baker had very evidently been shot. Inferior to the right scapula were elliptical wounds compatible with an entry and exit gunshot wound. We chalk-outlined his body so that its positioning could be properly documented. I then rolled the body over and observed an entry bullet wound on the right neck slightly anterior to the angle of the mandible. I found another entry wound in the upper right chest wall, and one more entry wound in the right shoulder. There was visible blood on Mr. Baker's torso. Detective Lee of the sheriff's department was present and informed me that Lee had removed a knife from Mr. Baker's right hand, which was under his torso. I noticed there was blood in the palm of Mr. Baker's right hand. Detective Lee said that the knife also had blood on the handle in the area, where the hand would grip the knife.

I immediately questioned whether Mr. Baker was holding the knife when shot, since in my professional experience, a person who is gripping a knife when shot and is still holding the knife when he expires would normally not have blood on the palm or the knife handle, as the grip would generally insulate both areas from blood. This is called a void. A void occurs when a person's body or an object blocks a particular area such that blood cannot get on or into that area. As a result, when the body or object is removed, there is an empty space that is void of blood. Hence the term, "void."

While I was at Ashgate, I saw the defendant, who was being detained by Detective Lee and a sheriff's deputy. I looked at her left arm, which had some three to four superficial, shallow scratches or knife cuts that were clustered in one spot and parallel to each other. They were not deep and were consistent with wounds that had been self-inflicted. None was life threatening in any way. They were not actively bleeding and did not require sutures or bandaging.

Deputy Coroner Beazley took custody of the body, placing it in a body bag, and we returned with the body to the coroner's office. When we arrived, Kelly Baker's body was placed in the morgue. Later that day Detective Lee , with my permission, took a full set of fingerprints and Mr. Baker's robe and pajamas. At Lee's request, I took a vial of blood from Mr. Baker's body, sealed it, and gave it to Detective Lee as evidence.

I performed a general autopsy examination on the body of Kelly Baker at the Darrow County Coroner's Office on September 8, YR-1, at approximately 8:30 a.m. Kelly Baker was forty-two years old, six feet in height, weighed 170 pounds, and had light brown hair and brown eyes. He showed no external evidence of trauma other than the bullet wounds, which I will describe in detail.

I then performed an internal examination. I found no evidence of trauma, illness, or any other factor that would contribute to the cause of death other than gunshot wounds of the neck and thorax. Mr. Baker was shot four times. I will describe these wounds by referring to them as wounds one, two, three, and four, but that is not necessarily the order in which they entered the body. There is no way to medically decipher the exact order of the gunshots. Wound number one entered Mr. Baker's face on the right side eight inches below the top of his head. The wound track led backward, downward, and leftward. The bullet perforated the right carotid artery, causing significant bleeding. I located a bullet that was deformed from subcutaneous tissue in his back approximately ten inches below the top of his head. I turned over possession of the recovered bullet to Detective Lee early that afternoon.

Wound number two entered Mr. Baker's right upper chest right of the midline. The wound track traveled backward, downward, and leftward, perforating both the right upper and lower lung lobes, the pulmonary arteries, the left upper and lower lung lobes, and exited the back about five inches lower than it entered and about a foot left of the entrance wound. This wound also caused considerable bleeding.

Wound number three entered Mr. Baker's right shoulder about ten inches below the top of his head and about seven inches to the right of the front midline. This wound track also traveled backward, downward, and leftward and perforated the head of his left humerus, which is the upper arm bone. The wound track perforated the cervical vertebra number five, the left clavicle, and came to a stop just in front of the head of the left humerus. I recovered a deformed bullet, which I later turned over to Detective Lee.

Wound number four entered Mr. Baker's right back about one-and-a-half feet below the top of his head and about four inches to the right of the midline. This wound track traveled downward and leftward, traversing to the right back where it exited at about the same distance from the top of the head about two inches to the right of the midline. In layperson's terms, this type of shot would be called a "graze."

I did not detect any muzzle burns or gun powder debris at the entry site or in the wound track of any of the four wounds. This would indicate that the shots were not fired from a close distance. I was present when Investigator Rodriguez swabbed Kelly Baker's body for gunshot power residue and did not detect any. I am also aware that there was no gunshot powder residue found on any of his clothing. This is consistent with Mr. Baker having been shot from at least four feet away, or more. Assuming that Mr. Baker was attacking Mrs. Baker with a knife and was able to get close enough to inflict knife wounds to her left arm, I would certainly expect to find powder debris on his body or clothing under such a factual scenario.

In my professional opinion, death occurred sometime between 8:00 and 8:30 a.m. and Mr. Baker was in a seated position when he was shot multiple times. I base this opinion on the downward angle and the right to left trajectory of the gunshot wounds, which are also consistent with the positioning of the various blood stains and spatter found throughout the scene, and the distance and angle of where the pistol and shell casings were located to where Mr. Baker's body was found. It is my professional opinion to a reasonable degree of medical certainty that Mr. Baker was seated at the table in the chair facing the TV having breakfast when he was shot.

CROSS-EXAMINATION

There is no medical certification one can acquire to become an expert in gunshot wound deaths or trajectory analysis. There are no specific courses given in medical school dealing specifically with these areas. The position of the wound tracks leading from a higher to a lower position on the body of Mr. Baker indicate that Mr. Baker's head and torso were in an upright position with his body at lower level than the shooter, such as in a seated position. It is true that if Mr. Baker was standing in a semicrouch position facing Mrs. Baker, then the wound tracks for wounds numbered one, two, three, and four would be consistent with such a position if he spun his body to his left as she began to shoot, causing the right side of his face, chest, shoulder, and back to be closest to the gun. This positioning would have allowed the trajectory of the bullets to travel in a downward direction and across his body from right to left. However, the absence of blood spatter on the table and absence of saliva in the blood that was found undermines this scenario because if Mr. Baker was shot in the face and upper body while spinning to his left, we would expect to see blood spatter on the table, and it would likely have at least some saliva in it. I am aware that, if Mr. Baker was standing in a semi-couched position when shot, we do not know for sure where exactly he was standing. I am also aware that if a gunshot does not exit the body, there may not be high-velocity blood spatter observed from that particular gun shot.

I examined the G.I. tract and found contents in the stomach, but I cannot tell you whether the contents were from a croissant or coffee. I am not aware that any effort was made by law enforcement to determine what, if any, contents were in Mr. Baker's stomach that morning.

My practice has included studies in the field of the effects of alcohol on the human body and mind, observing individuals in various stages of intoxication, correlating their behavior with blood alcohol levels, and on occasion testifying in court concerning my findings and conclusions in individual cases. I have been found by courts to be an expert in this field on at least five occasions. The blood sample taken from Mr. Baker was found by analysis to contain .08 percent alcohol by weight. While individuals vary as to their ability to function at different blood alcohol levels, in my opinion all people would be appreciably impaired by alcohol at .08 percent sufficiently that they could not safely operate a motor vehicle, which is why the legal limit to operate a motor vehicle in all states, including Nita, is .08 percent. Certainly, all persons would have significant impairment of judgment, of visual acuity, of physical coordination, and of general perception of events. It is also not unusual for one who generally has an even disposition and temper to become combative and violent when under the influence of alcohol. I have seen this change in behavior in many individuals and have read definitive studies in the field that substantiate this. I am familiar with the concepts of absorption and dissipation or burn-off as they relate to alcohol ingestion. It is true that the alcohol percentage in Mr. Baker's body does not tell us when he drank the alcohol. He could have consumed the alcohol sometime shortly before the shooting or he could have consumed it several hours before. If he had consumed it several hours before, he would have burned off alcohol at a rate somewhere around .02 percent per hour. If he had his last drink the night before around midnight, his blood alcohol level could well have been in the neighborhood of .20 or higher around 1:00 a.m. It would certainly be possible for someone with a .20 blood alcohol level to have greatly impaired judgment, and some people at that level are capable of harboring violent thoughts.

I do know Dr. Leslie Torres. I am aware Dr. Torres has called our office about this case. Dr. Torres was a professional associate in the Darrow County Coroner's Office for about three years and then moved to Marshall City. Dr. Torres apparently was unhappy at not being promoted to director of the Coroner's Office Pathology Laboratory. I have attended meetings of pathologists where Dr. Torres has been discussed. Dr. Torres has apparently said that they know more than any of the pathologists in Nita and should have been made the director of the laboratory. I am aware of Dr. Torres's opinion in this case, and in my professional medical opinion, Dr. Torres's opinion is incorrect.

I have reviewed the foregoing and it is a true and correct transcription of my testimony on October 20, YR-1, at the preliminary hearing in State v. Baker, in the Darrow County District Court, Nita City, Nita.

Morgan P. Kahn

Morgan P. Kahn, MD
Medical Examiner and Forensic Pathologist
Darrow County, Nita

Testimony of Kit Manville at Preliminary Hearing

Oath Administered

Direct Examination

I live at 19925 Talbot Road in Darrow County, about ten miles north of Warrenton. I am a farrier and a musician and singer. For about two years, I worked for Sarah Baker at Ashgate Farm. Then Ms. Baker fired me because she was afraid I knew too much about her cheating on her husband.

For over a year, I was very happy at Ashgate. Everyone treated me well, and I was constantly praised by the Bakers and by the manager, Chris Spanalski. I made several recommendations that changed the system of shoeing the horses and caring for them. Also, I was constantly asked to entertain at the Ashgate parties. I played the guitar and sang folk and bluegrass songs. Mr. Baker told me that I was the best thing that happened to their polo pony raising program.

I did witness Ms. Baker in a pretty violent incident about a year and a half ago. After that incident, Ms. Baker's attitude toward me changed. The whole thing stemmed over a customer, Will White, who was upset because his pony died shortly after he bought it from Ashgate. He came to Ashgate about seven in the evening. I was still working, and he stopped and asked me where Ms. Baker was. I could tell that he was perturbed, so after I told him where the Ashgate residence was, I walked over there to make sure things were okay. I saw White go to the door and then Ms. Baker walked out. She started shouting right away. She told him to get off the property. He walked away and said something about suing her. She ran into the house and came out with a gun. I could see her pointing the gun in his direction, and then I heard a loud bang. I thought maybe she had shot him, but then I saw Mr. White run away. I remember her saying something like, "Next time you come here you're going to be carried out."

As Mr. White got into his car, Ms. Baker walked back into the house. About five minutes later she came back out and headed down to where I was finishing my work. I saw her coming and walked out to meet her. She said, "You know, Kit, we at Ashgate have to stick together. That's part of being part of the Ashgate family. You know that man was going to attack me. I had to defend myself. My daddy a long time ago showed me how to protect myself. That's why I have what he calls 'the equalizer,' a 9mm equalizer." I just nodded. She said that I should talk to Chris Spanalski, and Chris would explain how to deal with the sheriff's office if there were any questions. She walked off. A little later the sheriff's deputies arrived and talked to me. I wasn't sure what to do, but I told them that White was really angry and maybe Ms. Baker thought she needed to protect herself.

I guess Ms. Baker thought that I told the sheriff's office everything, because after that she wouldn't talk to me. Her attorney talked to me once, and I told her the same thing. I don't know exactly what happened with her case, but I understand she got some kind of a fine.

Shortly after that, Chris Spanalski called me into the manager's office and told me that I was being disciplined for drinking on the job and that my employment record would show that. I told Chris that I did not drink on the job, and the only time that I had alcoholic drinks at Ashgate was either when I was entertaining at their parties or when Mr. Baker would invite me to have a drink. Actually, Mr. Baker and I did this pretty often. We were good friends. We liked to drink and bet on horses together. Mr. Baker actually bailed me out of a pretty bad debt I owed a bookie—five grand! Probably saved me from a good beating. I appreciated that man and I'm going to miss him. Recently I had actually started to rack up some more debt with another bookie—vices, right?—and owed him $1,500. Mr. Baker promised he would help me out, but that bitch killed him before he was able to give me the money. I really hate her. Sorry, she just makes me so mad. Anyway, back to the story. Mr. Baker and I would go down to the track as often as we could to make some extra cash. Ms. Baker controlled all her money and kept Mr. Baker on a strict allowance. He hated it but didn't want to give up his fancy lifestyle. Mr. Baker was really lonely this last year because Ms. Baker wasn't paying much attention to him. It hurt his ego. He told me often that he wanted to "man up" and "show her who was boss," but he was worried she would kick him out and he'd lose access to her money. Mr. Baker would often ask me over drinks what was happening on the farm, and I would give him the latest. I thought he ought to know that Ms. Baker was playing around on him. She was spending a lot of time with someone else, some DA. I saw them together at Ashgate. She sure gave this person looks she didn't give her husband, if you know what I mean.

The first time I saw the two together was at the Community Games. Usually, Ms. Baker and Mr. Baker would be in the family box seats. This time Mr. Baker wasn't there, and she was with the DA. I think it raised a few eyebrows, but after the games, a lot of the people who came to the games went over to The Saddle, a fancy restaurant in Warrenton. I was there with some friends, and I saw Ms. Baker and the DA sitting by themselves in a corner booth. I watched them pretty closely because she was acting funny. They kept touching and moving closer together. She would laugh and put her hand on the DA's body. She never acted that way with Mr. Baker.

I think the worst time was about two months ago when I saw Ms. Baker and the DA get out of her fancy Lexus. I was down the road at the barn, but I could see them and hear them. They both looked around, as if to see if anyone was there, and then they walked toward the house. She had her head on the DA's shoulder. I could hear her saying something like, "I just love the way you are, Kendall." They hugged and walked into the house. I could hear her laughing. I knew something was up. Maybe an hour later they came out. I was still in the shop, maybe 100 feet away, and I could see that they had been up to something, because her hair was really messed up. They got into the Lexus and drove off. I could see that she was putting lipstick on as they drove away.

It was getting to the point where they were making a sucker out of poor Mr. Baker. The last straw was about a week later when I heard Ms. Baker and Chris Spanalski talking next door. Ms. Baker was telling Chris something about cutting Mr. Baker out of the will. I believe the words she used were, "I've decided Kelly is out of the will. Don't worry, I am still leaving your house to you. If Kelly gives me any trouble, I know how to take care of him."

I waited until the next day, and then I called Mr. Baker and told him what I had heard. He seemed very surprised but then said something like, "It's OK, Kit, I could see this coming. You are a true friend. Don't worry, I won't forget it." He then told me that he was not going to give her a divorce unless she gave him his fair share of the property. He said she would have to take him to court, and he had talked to a lawyer, and the lawyer had said that they had a case, and it would cost Ms. Baker "millions." He said he was going to tell her that. I think that was the last time I ever talked to Mr. Baker.

In just a matter of a few days Chris Spanalski fired me and said that Ms. Baker was giving me three months' severance pay even though I wasn't entitled to it. I demanded to know why I was being fired, and Spanalski told me that I had a real alcohol problem, and it was affecting my work. That was a big lie. The whole thing was a cover-up to discredit me and what I knew to be true.

CROSS-EXAMINATION

It's true that Mr. Baker was upset at what was happening with this DA. Very upset. Every time I told him about one of those incidents, he would get really upset and would have several more drinks. I tried to make him feel better by telling him that he was the good guy here and that he was really getting a raw deal. I was never in the house when Ms. Baker and the person she called "Kendall" were there. I guess I couldn't say for sure from just seeing them together that they were definitely engaged in romantic conduct, but it certainly didn't look good. I know that I heard her say the word "love," but I can't be sure that it wasn't something like, "I love the things you say" or "I love the things you do." I can't remember whether they were carrying papers when they went in the door to the house.

I called Kelly Baker and told him that I had seen Ms. Baker and this DA at The Saddle restaurant. I thought he ought to know. I have no idea whether Ms. Baker had already told Mr. Baker about inviting the DA to the Community Games or whether she told him about the restaurant.

It is true that I have had a drinking problem that led to three DUI convictions, but I have kept my drinking separate from my work at Ashgate.

I had a little problem a while back when I loaned out an animal that wasn't mine. You see, I used to work for Barrett Farms, another farm in Nita, and I still have friends who work there. A buddy of mine who used to be in charge of their stables called me one weekend and asked me if I wanted to make a little extra cash on the side. I mean, who doesn't, right? Anyway, apparently a particular owner had left a horse there for boarding and grooming. She was going to be out of the country for several weeks, so my buddy and I loaned it out to another customer and split the cash proceeds. We charged the customer $1,000 to use the horse for the week and then split the proceeds $500 each. I guess what happened was the owner came back and somehow found out that her horse had been loaned out. She was pretty mad and reported it to the sheriff's department. I pled guilty and paid a fine. Looking back, it was a stupid thing to do, but it seemed like a good idea at the time.

I have reviewed the foregoing and it is a true and correct transcription of my testimony on October 20, YR-1, at the preliminary hearing in State v. Baker, in the Darrow County District Court, Nita City, Nita.

Kit Manville

Kit Manville

Statement of Chris Spanalski to Defense Investigator

I live at 8718 Springs Road in Warrenton, directly down the road from the Ashgate residence at Ashgate Farm. I am the manager of Ashgate Farm. I have worked for Sarah Baker since YR-18, and I knew her for at least three years before I became the manager. I graduated from Nita University in YR-21 with a degree in business. My family has been interested in polo for decades, and as a child I rode horses and watched my father play polo and my brother play polo. After graduating, I worked for Thompson Farms as an assistant manager, and in YR-18 Sarah Baker offered me the job of manager at Ashgate. My duties include direct responsibility for overseeing the entire operations, including the renting of facilities for polo, raising polo ponies, and providing polo and horse-riding lessons. Ashgate Farm employs approximately thirty staff, fifteen of whom are full time. I am responsible for everyone and everything on the farm. I spend twenty-four hours a day, seven days a week at the farm because I live and work on the property. It's pretty much my entire life.

Sarah Baker is one of the most gentle and caring people I know. She is scrupulously honest and very loyal and supportive to her employees. I could not have a better employer, and I consider her a true friend. She is beautiful, inside and out. To me, she is perfect.

About five years ago Sarah met Kelly Baker and was very impressed with him. She had been holding out for "someone perfect." They began to see a lot of each other, and often he came to the farm. Initially I liked him. He was personable, and he seemed to care very much for Sarah. However, he was at a party following a match one night when he had too much to drink, and he really got nasty. He uttered a few obscenities and refused to go home with Sarah. It was so embarrassing that most everyone left. I think that was shortly after they got married because after Sarah and Mr. Baker got married, I began to notice a change in their relationship. During the year before their marriage, they were always happy together. But gradually after their marriage they became more distant. Mr. Baker seemed to be gone most of the time. I really didn't see him that often, and when I did, he usually didn't stop to talk to me. He just ignored me. I began to worry about Sarah. She's very sensitive, and I knew that this must be bothering her, but I wasn't going to say anything unless she talked to me. Sarah and I worked very closely together, so I had plenty of opportunities to see the change in her. Lately she has seemed lonely and sad.

About a week before the shooting, I remember that Sarah was especially sad. In fact, she looked like she had been crying. I asked her if she was all right, and she said that she was sad because Kelly had broken one of her family treasures, a China lamp. I said something like, "Maybe you can find another like it." She said, "I'm not even sure I want to replace it after what he did." She then started sobbing really hard and said, "He threw it so hard against the fireplace that it shattered into like a million pieces! Drunken jerk!"

The times that Sarah seemed most happy in the last year were when she was working on Project WEB. She told me several times that she was blessed with a fortune, and she had a responsibility to help others less fortunate. She thought that Project WEB was one way to do that. Sarah for years has been holding charity events at Ashgate, and now she saw an opportunity to do that and tie it in with a community effort to build a home and center for abused women. She worked with a number of people including county officials. One was named Kendall Johnson. Johnson seemed very interested in helping and was at Ashgate a number of times helping to plan events. I think Sarah was her happiest in the last year when the two of them were making progress on the Center. She talked about that quite often. It wasn't anything romantic. They just shared a very strong common interest in Project WEB.

The first time I personally saw anything really wrong with Sarah and Mr. Baker was the night before the shooting. Sarah and I were going over some business matters at her home. We had just finished about 7:00 p.m. and were talking on the front porch. Mr. Baker drove up, parked his car directly in front of the porch, and walked over. He gave me a dirty look and then looked at Sarah and said something about the will. He looked really mad—scowling and yelling. Sarah hung her head and slumped her shoulders. She seemed embarrassed and looked over at me. Mr. Baker didn't look at me and spoke aggressively toward Sarah, demanding she give him an answer "right now" about her will. I left as quickly as I could. I was worried about Sarah, but I didn't think it was my place to interfere.

The next morning, I was in the business office, which is at the front of my home. I got a call from Sarah at 8:30 a.m. I know the time because I had a telephone appointment at 8:15, and I had just completed the call. Sarah was crying. She said that something terrible had happened and asked that I come immediately. I ran to her house. Sarah was on the porch with her hands over her face crying. She had blood on her arm, and I could see several cuts still bleeding. I asked her what happened. Sarah said Mr. Baker went crazy and told her that he was going to kill her. She said that Mr. Baker pointed a gun at her, and she was able to convince him to put it down. Then he got a kitchen knife and tried to slash her. We walked into the house and Sarah said, "I had to do it. He would have killed me." I saw Mr. Baker lying on the floor. He was holding a knife. He looked like he was dead. The kitchen was a bloody mess. The gun was lying on the floor. Sarah then said she had to call 911 and went over to the phone and called. Soon the sheriffs arrived.

I am not surprised that Mr. Baker was angry. If he was anything like he was the night before, then he was out of control. Poor Sarah. This whole experience has been horrible for her. First, she was nearly killed, and if she hadn't defended herself, she would have been. Now she has been falsely accused of murder. Fortunately, Johnson has been calling her and supporting her. Sarah has said several times that she didn't know how she would get through this without Kendall's help.

About a year after I came to work at Ashgate, one of the employees, a clerk, claimed I was altering the books and pocketing money. She was disgruntled because she had not been promoted, and she didn't like me from the day I arrived. I was arrested by the sheriff's office. I explained the whole thing to Sarah, and she immediately went down to the sheriff's office and told them that it was a big mistake. They dropped the charges. Obviously, the clerk had to be discharged for making false accusations. The clerk later filed suit for wrongful discharge, and it was settled for a nuisance value of $10,000.

Four years ago, I was falsely accused of diverting employment benefits. The whole matter was simply a big mistake. Two employees claimed that I had not been paying the premium on our employer-paid disability benefits package, but instead pocketing the money, and when they got hurt on the job and tried to make a claim, they were denied. There was some confusion over whether they were even eligible for that benefit in the first place and whether it was part of their employment package, but my attorney recommended that I plead guilty in exchange for straight probation and a fine. I took the attorney's advice and pled, but in thinking about it, I probably should have fought it. They were both friends of the clerk that had me arrested two years before. But through it all, Sarah has stuck by me, and for that, I'll always be grateful.

I have read the above statement, and it is true and correct.

Signed: *Chris Spanalski* Date: October 14, YR-1

Chris Spanalski

Witnessed: *Baxter Franklin* Date: October 14, YR-1

Baxter Franklin, Defense Investigator

Statement of Kendall Johnson to Defense Investigator

I am the chief deputy district attorney for Darrow County. I have been a prosecuting attorney for seventeen years and the chief deputy for the last five years. My career as a prosecuting attorney is very important to me. For as long as I can remember, I have wanted to be a DA. I grew up in a tough neighborhood in Nita City. I remember feeling hopeless, and I remember seeing my mother beaten by my drunken father. It left a lasting impression on me. As a prosecuting attorney, I had an opportunity to do something for all the people of our community, including the poor people. The present district attorney, Amara Okeke, has announced her plans to run for the state senate, and I have been urged to run for district attorney in two years. I live in Nita City and am single. I was divorced two years ago. I am fifty years old.

Sarah Baker and I are professional colleagues in the sense that we have worked together on community projects. I want to stress very strongly that while we are certainly good friends, there is absolutely no romantic relationship at all. I believe very strongly in what Sarah is trying to do for battered women, and I have worked very hard to help her. It is true that we have many common interests. I have a very keen interest in polo. I learned to play polo when I got a scholarship to a prep school, St. Michael's Academy. Then when I got a scholarship to Stanford, I joined the polo team. After college and law school I played as an amateur for The Grounders, one of the established polo teams in Darrow County.

I first met Sarah at a meeting of the Darrow County Battered Women Council about a year ago. County officials and community leaders were present. Sarah was introduced to me as the director of Project WEB. I knew who she was and knew of her interest in polo, and I knew that she held charity events at Ashgate. I suggested to her that funding for a battered women center could be developed through events at Ashgate. She liked the idea and told me that the Community Games were being held in a couple of months and asked for my help on the council in getting approval for directing some of the funds to the proposed Project WEB Center. I agreed. Later the council approved the plan.

Sarah invited me to attend the games as a guest, and after the games, we talked about our plans for the Center. Sarah suggested that we finish our discussion over dinner at The Saddle, an upscale restaurant in Warrenton. A number of the people who attended the games were present. Apparently, someone reported back to Kelly Baker about seeing us at the restaurant. I later got a call from Sarah informing me that Kelly was really upset and accused her of having an affair. I told her that I would be happy to talk with Kelly and explain, but she said not to worry, she would take care of it. The next time I talked with Sarah, about two weeks later, she said there was no problem with Kelly as she had taken care of it. For that reason, I did not worry about continuing to meet Sarah at Ashgate.

We met several more times at Ashgate. The passage you read me from Detective Lee's statement of someone named Manville is not correct. That's not the way it happened. It was about three weeks ago. Sarah picked me up at my office, as we had to go over plans she had developed for the Center, and the plans were at Ashgate. We were there for only about one hour, and it was all business. I don't remember talking outside the house, although we could have, but I know that Sarah's hair was not messed up. I have never seen her when she wasn't perfectly put together.

I explained to Detective Lee that my messages to Sarah were nothing more than just friendly banter. Sure, maybe we flirted a little sometimes, but who doesn't? We never had any physical contact and certainly never slept together. My message about things being tough was just an effort to encourage her to keep her spirits up and continue her good work in Project WEB. I have great admiration for Sarah, and I would happily serve as a character witness for her in any upcoming trial. I do not believe for a moment that she would ever commit murder—I've only ever known her to be peaceful, patient, and kind. If she killed Kelly Baker, then she did it only to protect herself. It is true that I have continued to offer my support to Sarah by calling her while this case has been pending. Anyone who felt the way I do about Sarah would do the same.

I have read the above statement consisting of two pages, and it is true and correct.

Signed: *Kendall Johnson* Date: October 14, YR-1

Kendall Johnson

Witnessed: *Baxter Franklin* Date: October 14, YR-1

Baxter Franklin, Defense Investigator

Northern Nita Forensic Pathology Laboratories
St. Luke's Medical Building, Suite 410
1601 Heffernan Drive
Marshall City, Nita 55059
(819) 555-6066

December 18, YR-1

Clifford Berres, Esq.
Masi Berres & Shoun
868 Stock Drive
Nita City, Nita 55058

Re: Forensic Analysis

Dear Mr. Berres:

Thank you for referring Ms. Baker's case. As you requested, I have reviewed all the materials in this case and come to opinions with regard to the position of Kelly Baker when he was shot; Sarah Baker's wounds; and the presence of blood on Kelly Baker's right palm and the knife handle. I have come to my opinions to a reasonable degree of medical certainty. I have enclosed a copy of my curriculum vitae.

Position of Kelly Baker When Shot

After careful review of the autopsy protocol by Dr. Morgan Kahn, no major inconsistencies are found that would in any way preclude the possibility, if not probability, that the decedent Kelly Baker was advancing toward Ms. Baker and attacking her when the shots were fired. Rarely is there definite anatomic evidence to support the position of the body in relation to a specific injury given the number of variables that must be taken into consideration. For example, without knowing the exact order of the gunshot wounds and whether the decedent Kelly Baker was trying to "twist" out of the way, no definite opinions can be made as to the exact location of the body in relation to the weapon.

Gunshot wound labeled as number four in the autopsy report is of special interest. This wound, which is a grazing injury, shows the entrance and exit wound to be at the same level, which is to say, horizontally oriented. If the decedent was in a sitting position and Ms. Baker in a standing position when this shot was fired then the weapon had to be fired while being held at waist level (firing from the hip). This would be a most awkward position to shoot a gun. And very inaccurate, particularly for someone like Ms. Baker who is 5'9". Further, given that Ms. Baker is the daughter of an international arms dealer, I would presume that she would know how to properly shoot a gun. Also, the trajectories of the remaining projectiles appear to travel in a downward trajectory across the body, from right to left. Again, if the decedent was sitting, it would be more plausible for the wounds to travel from front to back rather than from right to left.

I agree that because no power residue was found on Mr. Baker's body or clothes, his body had to have been at least four feet away from the gun at the time it was fired. However, the knife was not tested for gunshot powder residue, so we cannot know for sure that it was not within four feet of the gun. Further, it is possible that the reason no blood was found on the kitchen table is because Mr. Baker was not in front of the table when the two perforating gunshot wounds exited his body. Mr. Baker could have attacked with a knife in a crouched position and been shot repeatedly as he twisted his body to the left, exposing his right side, and then fell in the area of the chair. The blood spatter found on the chair is consistent with the forceful expectoration of blood from the body of Kelly Baker as he twisted and fell to the ground from the force of the gunshots. In fact, the downward and right-to-left bullet trajectory would make sense if the shots were fired and struck Mr. Baker in the order set forth in Dr. Kahn's autopsy report (1, 2, 3, then 4). Further, the lack of saliva in the blood on the chair makes sense given that the gunshot to the mouth was not a perforating wound.

Dannie Rodriguez has concluded through a trajectory analysis that Mr. Baker was seated when he was shot. First, there is evidence that Mr. Baker was standing upright during some of the blood loss based on the elongated bloodstains on the front thighs of his pajama pants, consistent with a standing position. Second, Dannie Rodriguez did not take sufficient measurements to make a positive trajectory conclusion. We do not even know the length of Mr. Baker's torso in order to determine how tall his body would have been when sitting in a chair seat that measured 18 inches from the floor. Further, neither the casings nor the body were at the scene when he conducted his investigation. An alternative explanation of the observed facts would be that Mr. Baker was standing but crouched as he approached Ms. Baker with the knife in his right hand. Her being 5'9", shooting him while he was in a crouched position (a downward angle), and at a distance greater than 4 feet could result in blood spatter that would be measured at forty-two to forty-six inches from the floor and could result in the bullets striking the east wall at thirty-one to thirty-three inches off the floor. Other alternatives can also be supported, including that Mr. Baker was in a standing, crouched position approaching Ms. Baker with the knife in his hand and tried to spin out of the way when Ms. Baker fired her first shot, which could have caused the grazing back injury. At that point Mr. Baker, being unsteady/uncoordinated due to his .08 BAC, could have fallen to his knees causing the subsequent shots to hit him at a downward angle. It is my opinion, to a reasonable degree of medical certainty, that Mr. Baker's injuries are consistent with him standing, presenting his right side to Ms. Baker in a crouched position with his upper torso bent slightly forward while wielding a knife in his right hand at the time he was shot.

Sarah Baker's Wounds

I have reviewed Dr. Kahn's autopsy report concerning Sarah Baker's wounds, and I am not aware of any scientific basis or literature that would confirm or deny Dr. Kahn's supposition that the wounds on Sarah Baker were self-inflicted. I know of no way to prove one way or the other that the wounds were self-inflicted or caused by another; all that can be said is that they are consistent with incised, superficial wounds.

Presence of Blood on Kelly Baker's Right Palm and the Knife

In my experience as a forensic pathologist, I have personally reviewed cases where the deceased was holding a knife and suffered fatal injuries. I have seen cases where the hand and the knife were blood free and other cases where the hand and knife had the decedent's blood on both. There are a number of factors that could affect the outcome, including the tension with which the knife was held at death. It is clearly possible that the grip of the decedent relaxed prior to death, allowing blood from his body to infiltrate the palm of the hand and the knife's handle.

Conclusion

While it is impossible from my review of the case to say that any or all of the facts positively prove any one factual scenario in this case, I can say that there is a reasonable possibility that Sarah Baker fired the pistol in an effort to protect herself from a knife attack by Kelly Baker, a possibility at least as reasonable as the theory that Kelly Baker was in a seated position.

Additional Background Information

There are a few areas that need amplification. I have examined hundreds of bodies at death scenes of all kinds as well as a number of homicide scenes after the body was transported. I have performed over 2,000 medicolegal autopsies and have supervised another 100–150. At least 35 percent of those cases involved gunshot wounds. I have qualified and testified as an expert witness in the states of Nita and California and in federal courts over 100 times. I have appeared in criminal proceedings for both the prosecution and defense and have been retained by plaintiff's and defense attorneys in civil matters. The areas of my testimony have included cause of death, natural disease, and the nature and causation of various injuries present in both deceased and surviving persons, including gunshot and knife wounds and crime scene reconstruction. I have rendered an expert opinion in court concerning gunshot wounds in approximately forty-five cases. I have also been involved in interpreting results of serology and toxicology testing. Northern Nita Forensic Pathology Laboratories provides forensic pathology services for Marshall County. I currently perform thirty to forty autopsies per month. I have consulted for private attorneys, public defenders, and district attorneys in several dozen cases.

If I testify as an expert in this case, you should know that Dr. Morgan Kahn and I once worked together in the Darrow County Coroner's Office. When Dr. Kahn was appointed Medical Director of that office, I chose to leave and come to Marshall City with Northern Nita Forensic Pathology Laboratories. While I respect Dr. Kahn's medical qualifications and ability, I found it difficult, as a number of other medical associates did, to work with Dr. Kahn. Since then, I have testified on a number of occasions in opposition to the conclusions of Dr. Kahn. Unfortunately, Dr. Kahn has not accepted well my contrary opinions and has attempted to bring into question my objectivity, competence, and ethics by filing a complaint with the American Board of Pathology. Dr. Kahn contended in the complaint that I had altered a tissue specimen in an alleged jail suicide case where I had concluded that the inmate had been beaten by others, possibly jail personnel, before a rope was placed around his neck. Although the matter is pending, I have no doubt that the board will find the complaint groundless, as I have positive proof of the condition of the tissue specimen when I inspected it, because I photographed the specimen before concluding my examination. I don't believe Dr. Kahn is aware of this proof.

To date I have devoted eight hours in case review, analysis, and the preparation of this report at the standard rate of $350 per hour for a total of $2,800. Professional time devoted to preparing for and attending court will be billed at the same rate. If you require additional information or would like to discuss the case further, please feel free to call me.

Sincerely,

Leslie Torres

Leslie Torres, MD

Curriculum Vitae

Leslie Torres, MD
1601 Heffernan Drive, Suite 410
Marshall City, Nita 99915
(721) 555-6066
ltorres@nnfpl.nita

EDUCATIONAL BACKGROUND

- BS, with great distinction in Biology and Chemistry, Charleston Southern University, YR-14 MD, fourth in class, Medical University of South Carolina, YR-13
- Residency in Anatomical and Clinical Pathology, University of California–Davis, YR-13 to YR-9

EMPLOYMENT HISTORY

- Forensic Pathologist, Los Angeles Coroner's Office, YR-9 to YR-6
- Forensic Pathologist, Darrow County Coroner's Office, YR-6 to YR-4
- Assistant Medical Director, Darrow County Coroner's Office, YR-4 to YR-3
- Forensic Pathologist, Northern Nita Forensic Pathology Laboratories, YR-3 to present

CERTIFICATION AND LICENSURE

- Diplomate, National Board of Medical Examiners—July YR-12
- California Physician's and Surgeon's License—July YR-12
- American Board of Pathology—Anatomic/Clinical Pathology—November YR-9
- American Board of Pathology—Forensic Pathology—May YR-7
- Nita Physician's and Surgeon's License—June YR-6
- American Board of Forensic Examiners—September YR-1

TEACHING EXPERIENCE

- Assistant and Associate Professor of Pathology, Nita University, YR-6 to present
- Guest lecturer, University of California–Davis; Darrow Community College; Glenback College

PRESENTATIONS

- University of California–Davis—"Gunshot Wounds: Self-Defense or Murder?" May YR-6.
- Nita State Hospital—Fifth Annual Pathology Forum—"Forensic Aspects of Homicide," November YR-6.
- Marshall County Sheriff–Coroner's Death Investigation Course—"Introduction to Forensic Medicine," April 21, YR-1.

PUBLICATIONS

- Torres, L., "Securing Evidence in Gunshot Wound Deaths," *Journal of Forensic Sciences*, May 2011. Fernandez, D.E., and Torres, L., "Examination of Toxicological Evidence in Homicides," *Journal of Police Science*, October YR-4.
- Scheffing, L., "Objectivity vs. Advocacy," *Journal on Advocacy*, February YR-4.

COMMITTEE APPOINTMENTS

- LOS ANGELES COUNTY GUNSHOT DEATH REVIEW TEAM, YR-7–YR-6. Multidisciplinary review team charged with analyzing gunshot wound deaths and recommending investigative and teaching improvements in such cases.
- NITA SIDS PROTOCOL COMMITTEE, CONSULTANT, April YR-5 to YR-3. Committee responsible for producing final form of a sudden infant death syndrome autopsy protocol for Nita Department of Health, as mandated by Nita SB 1069.
- MARSHALL COUNTY TOXICOLOGY REVIEW TEAM, August YR-3 to present. Team formed as a pilot program sponsored by the State of Nita to investigate causes and recommend preventive strategies for mortality as a result of toxic substances.
- NORTHERN NITA REGIONAL TRAUMA QUALITY IMPROVEMENT COMMITTEE, July YR-3 to present. Reviews quality assurance for trauma care in Northern Nita counties.

Jury Instructions

PART I
PRELIMINARY INSTRUCTIONS GIVEN PRIOR TO EVIDENCE

1.00 INTRODUCTION

You have been selected as jurors and have taken an oath to well and truly try this case.

During the progress of the trial there will be periods of time when the court recesses. During those periods of time, you must not talk to any of the parties, their lawyers, or any of the witnesses.

If any attempt is made by anyone to talk to you concerning the matters here under consideration, you should immediately report that fact to the court.

You should keep an open mind. You should not form or express an opinion during the trial and should reach no conclusion in this case until you have heard all of the evidence, the arguments of counsel, and the final instructions as to the law that will be given to you by the court.

1.01 Conduct of the Trial

First, the attorneys will have an opportunity to make opening statements. These statements are not evidence and should be considered only as a preview of what the attorneys expect the evidence will be.

Following opening statements, witnesses will be called to testify. They will be placed under oath and questioned by the attorneys. Documents and other tangible exhibits may also be received as evidence. If an exhibit is given to you to examine, you should examine it carefully, individually, and without any comment.

It is counsel's right and duty to object when testimony or other evidence is being offered that counsel believes is not admissible.

When the court sustains an objection to a question, you must disregard the question and the answer, if one has been given, and draw no inference from the question or answer or speculate about what the witness would have said if permitted to answer. You must also disregard evidence stricken from the record.

When the court sustains an objection to any evidence, disregard that evidence. When the court overrules an objection to any evidence, you must not give that evidence any more weight than if the objection had not been made.

When the evidence is completed, the attorneys will make final statements. These final statements are not evidence but are given to assist you in evaluating the evidence. The attorneys are also permitted to argue in an attempt to persuade you to a particular verdict. You may accept or reject those arguments as you see fit.

Finally, just before you retire to consider your verdict, I will give you further instructions on the law that applies to this case.

PART II
FINAL INSTRUCTIONS

2.00 RESPECTIVE DUTIES OF JUDGE AND JURY

Ladies and Gentlemen of the Jury:

You have heard all the evidence and the arguments of the attorneys, and now it is my duty to instruct you on the law. You must arrive at your verdict by unanimous vote applying the law, as you are now instructed, to the facts as you find them to be.

The law applicable to this case is stated in these instructions, and it is your duty to follow all of them.

You must not single out certain instructions and disregard others.

It is your duty to determine the facts and to determine them only from the evidence in this case. You are to apply the law to the facts and in this way decide the case. You must not be governed or influenced by sympathy or prejudice for or against any party in this case. Your verdict must be based on evidence and not upon speculation, guess, or conjecture.

From time to time the court has ruled on the admissibility of evidence. You must not concern yourselves with the reasons for these rulings. You should disregard questions and exhibits that were withdrawn or to which objections were sustained.

You should also disregard testimony and exhibits that the court has refused or stricken.

The evidence that you should consider consists only of the witnesses' testimony and the exhibits the court has received.

Any evidence that was received for a limited purpose should not be considered by you for any other purpose.

You should consider all the evidence in the light of your own observations and experiences in life.

Neither by these instructions nor by any ruling or remark that I have made do I mean to indicate any opinion as to the facts or as to what your verdict should be.

2.01 Credibility of Witnesses

You are the sole judges of the credibility of the witnesses and of the weight to be given to the testimony of each witness. In determining what credit is to be given any witness, you may take into account the witness's ability and opportunity to observe; the manner and appearance while testifying; any interest, bias, or prejudice the witness may have; the reasonableness of the testimony considered in the light of all the evidence; and any other factors that bear on the believability and weight of the witness's testimony.

2.02 Believability of a Witness—Conviction of a Criminal Offense

The fact that a witness has been convicted of a criminal offense, if such be a fact, may be considered by you only for the purpose of determining the believability of that witness. The fact of such a conviction does not necessarily destroy or impair a witness's believability. It is one of the circumstances that you may take into consideration in weighing the testimony of such a witness.

2.03 Direct and Circumstantial Evidence

The law recognizes two kinds of evidence: direct and circumstantial. Direct evidence proves a fact directly; that is, the evidence by itself, if true, established the fact. Circumstantial evidence is the proof of facts or circumstances that give rise to a reasonable inference of other facts; that is, circumstantial evidence proves a fact indirectly in that it follows from other facts or circumstances according to common experience and observations in life. An eyewitness is a common example of direct evidence, while human footprints are circumstantial evidence that a person was present.

The law makes no distinction between direct and circumstantial evidence as to the degree or amount of proof required, and each should be considered according to whatever weight or value it may have. All of the evidence should be considered and evaluated by you in arriving at your verdict.

2.04 Charging Document—Criminal Indictment

The Criminal Indictment in this case is the formal method of accusing the defendant of a crime and placing her on trial. It is not any evidence against the defendant and does not create any inference or guilt. The State has the burden of proving beyond a reasonable doubt every essential element of the crimes charged in the Indictment.

2.05 Presumption of Innocence

The defendant is presumed to be innocent of the charges against her. This presumption remains with her throughout every stage of the trial and during your deliberations on the verdict. The presumption is not overcome until, from all the evidence in the case, you are convinced beyond a reasonable doubt that the defendant is guilty.

2.06 Burden of Proof

The State has the burden of proving the guilt of the defendant beyond a reasonable doubt, and this burden remains on the State throughout the case. The defendant is not required to prove her innocence.

2.07 Reasonable Doubt

Reasonable doubt means a doubt based upon reason and common sense that arises from a fair and rational consideration of all the evidence or lack of evidence in this case. It is a doubt that is not a vague, speculative, or imaginary doubt but such a doubt as would cause reasonable persons to hesitate to act in matters of importance to themselves.

2.08 Motive

Motive is not an element of the crimes charged and need not be shown. However, you may consider motive or lack of motive as a circumstance in this case. The presence of motive may tend to establish guilt. The absence of motive may tend to establish innocence. You will therefore give its presence or absence, as the case may be, the weight to which you find it to be entitled.

2.09 Defendant Not Testifying—No Inference of Guilt May Be Drawn

A defendant in a criminal trial has a constitutional right not to be compelled to testify. You must not draw any inference from the fact that a defendant does not testify. Further, you must neither discuss this matter nor permit it to enter into your deliberations in any way.

2.10 Expert Testimony

A person is qualified to testify as an expert if they have special knowledge, skill, experience, training, or education sufficient to qualify them as an expert on the subject to which the testimony relates.

You are not bound to accept an expert opinion as conclusive but should give it the weight to which you find it entitled. You may disregard any such opinion if you find it to be unreasonable.

3.00 CHARGES

The State of Nita has charged the defendant, Sarah Baker, with the crime of first-degree murder, which includes the lesser-included crimes of second-degree murder and voluntary manslaughter. If you are not satisfied beyond a reasonable doubt that the defendant is guilty of the crime charged, you may nevertheless convict the defendant of any lesser crime, if you are convinced beyond a reasonable doubt that the defendant is guilty of such lesser crime. The defendant has pleaded not guilty.

3.01 First-Degree Murder

Under the criminal code of the State of Nita a person commits the crime of first-degree murder if, with premeditation and the intent to cause the death of a person other than themselves, they cause the death of another person.

A person acts intentionally with respect to a result or to conduct described by a statute defining a crime when their conscious objective is to cause such result or to engage in such conduct.

Premeditation means that a deliberate decision to commit the act has been made after the exercise of reflection and judgment concerning the act. No specific plan or amount of time of reflection is required, but the facts must demonstrate a period of time long enough to allow reflection and thought by the defendant.

To sustain the charge of first-degree murder the State must prove:

1) that the defendant performed the acts that caused the death of Kelly Baker, and
2) that the defendant acted with premeditation and the intent to cause the death of Kelly Baker.

If you find from your consideration of all the evidence that each of these propositions has been proved beyond a reasonable doubt, then you should find the defendant guilty of first-degree murder.

If, on the other hand, you find from your consideration of all the evidence that any of these propositions has not been proved beyond a reasonable doubt, then you should find the defendant not guilty of first-degree murder.

3.02 Second-Degree Murder

Under the Criminal Code of the state of Nita a person commits the crime of second-degree murder if:

1) they intentionally, but not with premeditation, cause the death of a person, or
2) with intent to cause serious injury to a person other than themself, they cause the death of that person or of another person.

A person acts intentionally with respect to a result or to conduct described by a statute defining a crime when his or her conscious objective is to cause such result or to engage in such conduct.

To sustain the charge of second-degree murder, the State must prove the following propositions:

1) that the defendant performed the acts that caused the death of Kelly Baker, and
2) that the defendant intended to kill or cause serious bodily injury to Kelly Baker.

If you find from your consideration of all the evidence that each of these propositions has been proven beyond a reasonable doubt, then you should find the defendant guilty of second-degree murder.

If, on the other hand, you find from your consideration of all the evidence that any of these propositions has not been proved beyond a reasonable doubt, then you should find the defendant not guilty of second-degree murder.

3.03 Voluntary Manslaughter

Under the Criminal Code of the state of Nita, a person commits the crime of voluntary manslaughter if:

> They intentionally, but not after deliberation, cause the death of a person under circumstances where the act causing the death was performed upon a sudden heat of passion and inflammatory anger caused by a serious and highly provoking act of the intended victim, affecting the person killing sufficiently to excite an irresistible passion in a reasonable person. An example of a circumstance that could provoke such a sudden heat of passion or inflammatory anger could include walking in on a spouse engaged in an act of infidelity. However, if between the provocation and the killing there is an interval sufficient for the voice of reason and humanity to be heard, the killing is murder.

To sustain the charge of voluntary manslaughter the State must prove that the defendant intentionally caused the death of Kelly Baker under circumstances where the act causing death was performed upon a sudden heat of passion caused by a serious and highly provoking act of the intended victim, Kelly Baker.

If you find from your consideration of all the evidence that this proposition has been proved beyond a reasonable doubt, then you should find the defendant guilty of voluntary manslaughter.

If, on the other hand, you find from your consideration of all the evidence that this proposition has not been proved beyond a reasonable doubt, then you should find the defendant not guilty of voluntary manslaughter.

3.04 Self-Defense

The killing of another person in self-defense is justifiable and not unlawful when the person who does the killing actually and reasonably believes:

1) that there is imminent, immediate danger that the other person will either kill them or cause them great bodily harm, and
2) that it is necessary under the circumstances for them to use in self-defense such force or means as might cause the death of the other person for the purpose of avoiding death or great bodily injury to herself.

A mere fear of death or great bodily injury is not sufficient to justify a homicide. To justify taking the life of another in self-defense, the circumstances must be such as to excite the fears of a reasonable person placed in a similar position, and the party killing must act under the influence of such fears alone, not by hatred or any other emotion. Objectively, the danger must be apparent, present, immediate, and instantly dealt with so as to avoid bodily harm or death; and subjectively, the killing must be done under a well-founded belief that it is necessary to save oneself from death or great bodily harm.

If all of the above elements are satisfied, the actor has no duty to retreat and may act in self-defense.

The State has the burden to prove that the killing was not in lawful self-defense. If you have a reasonable doubt that such killing was unlawful, then you must find the defendant not guilty.

4.00 JURY MUST NOT CONSIDER PENALTY

In your deliberations, do not discuss or consider the subject of penalty or punishment. That subject must not in any way affect your verdict.

4.01 Concluding Instruction

You shall now retire and select one of your number to act as presiding juror. They will preside over your deliberations. In order to reach a verdict all jurors must agree to the decision. As soon as all of you have agreed upon a verdict, so that each may state truthfully that the verdict expresses their vote, have it dated and signed by your presiding juror and return with it to the courtroom.

Applicable Nita Criminal Code and Employment Code Sections

Section 100 N.C.C. Homicide, Definition of Terms

(1) Homicide means the killing of a person by another.

(2) Person, when referring to the victim of a homicide, means a human being who had been born and was alive at the time of the homicidal act.

(3) The term "with premeditation" means not only intentionally, but also that the decision to commit the act has been made after the exercise of reflection and judgment concerning the act. An act committed after deliberation is never one that has been committed in a hasty or impulsive manner.

Section 101 N.C.C. First-Degree Murder

(1) A person commits the crime of first-degree murder if, with premeditation and the intent to cause the death of a person other than themself, they cause the death of that person or of another person.

(2) If the first-degree murder was carried out for financial gain, or if the victim was a police officer, prosecutor, or judge, or if the murder was committed by means of a bomb, or if the defendant in this proceeding has been convicted of more than one offense of murder in the first degree, then the punishment shall be life without the possibility of parole.

(3) All other first-degree murder shall be punishable by confinement in prison for twenty-five years to life.

Section 102 N.C.C. Second-Degree Murder

(1) A person commits the crime of second-degree murder if:

(a) They intentionally, but not with premeditation, cause the death of a person, or

(b) With intent to cause serious bodily injury to a person other than themself, they cause the death of that person or of another person.

(2) Second-degree murder is punishable by confinement in prison for fifteen years to life.

Section 103 N.C.C. Voluntary Manslaughter

(1) A person commits the crime of voluntary manslaughter when they intentionally, but not after deliberation, cause the death of a person upon such a sudden heat of passion and inflammatory anger that any objective person in the same or similar circumstance would experience the same inflammatory anger to the point of forming intent to kill.

(2) Voluntary manslaughter is punishable by confinement in prison for five to fifteen years.

Section 104 N.C.C. Self-Defense

The killing of another person in self-defense is justifiable and not unlawful when the person who does the killing actually and reasonably believes there is imminent, immediate danger that the other person will either kill them or cause them great bodily harm, and that it is necessary under the circumstances to use in self-defense such force or means as might cause the death of another person for the purpose of avoiding death or great bodily injury.

To an objective person, the danger must be apparent, present, immediate, and instantly dealt with so as to avoid bodily harm or death; and to the subjective actor, the killing must be done under a well-founded fear and belief that it is necessary to immediately save oneself from death or great bodily harm.

The State has the burden to prove that any killing was not in lawful self-defense.

Section 242 N.C.C. Battery with a Dangerous Instrument

(1) Every person who commits, or attempts to commit, a battery with a dangerous instrument is guilty of a felony.

(2) A battery with a dangerous instrument is any willful and unlawful use of force or violence, or attempted use of the same, upon the person of another with any weapon or object capable of inflicting death or bodily injury.

(3) A battery with a dangerous instrument is punishable by confinement in prison for up to 10 years, or by a fine of up to $10,000, or both.

Section 490 N.C.C. Punishment for Theft

(1) Every person who is guilty of the theft of property of a value exceeding $500 is guilty of a felony punishable by confinement in prison for one to three years or by confinement in the county jail for up to one year.

(2) Theft in other cases is misdemeanor petty theft that is punishable by confinement in the county jail for up to six months, or by a fine of up to $1,000, or both.

Section 504 N.C.C. Embezzlement

(1) Every person who fraudulently appropriates to any use or purpose, not in the due and lawful execution of their trust, any property that that person possesses by virtue of trust, or secretes it with a fraudulent intent to appropriate it to such use or purpose, is guilty of embezzlement.

(2) Every person guilty of embezzlement is punishable in the manner prescribed for theft or property of the value embezzled.

Section 537c N.C.C. Fraudulent Loan of Animal

(1) Every owner, manager, proprietor, or other person, having the management, charge, access, or control of any livery stable, feed or boarding stable, who shall receive and take into their possession or control any horse, mule, or other animal belonging to any other

person, to be kept and cared for, and who shall then knowingly and fraudulently loan the same, without the consent or permission of the owner thereof, is guilty of a misdemeanor.

(2) A violation of this section is punishable by confinement in the county jail for up to 90 days, or by a fine of up to $500, or both.

Section 11357(b) N.C.C. Possession of Marijuana

(1) Every person who possesses not more than 28.5 grams of marijuana, other than concentrated cannabis, is guilty of a misdemeanor.

(2) A violation of this section is punishable by a fine of not more than $100.

Section 12031 N.C.C. Unlawful Discharge of a Firearm

(1) Every person who discharges a firearm in any public place or in any area of an incorporated city or an unincorporated territory not specifically designated for hunting is guilty of a misdemeanor.

(2) A violation of this section is punishable by confinement in county jail for up to 6 months, or by a fine of up to $1,000, or both.

Section 23152 N.C.C. Misdemeanor Driving Under the Influence—Alcohol or Drugs

(1) Any person who drives any vehicle under the influence of any alcoholic beverage or drug is guilty of a misdemeanor.

(2) Driving under the influence of alcohol or drugs is a misdemeanor punishable by confinement in the county jail for a period of not more than six months and by a fine of not less than $400 nor more than $1,000.

Section 27543 N.C.C. Tampering with Physical Evidence

A person is guilty of tampering with or fabricating physical evidence if, believing that a criminal investigation conducted by a law enforcement agency or an official proceeding is pending, or about to be instituted, such person:

(a) Alters, destroys, conceals, or removes any record, document, or thing with purpose to impair its verity or availability in such criminal investigation or official proceeding; or

(b) Makes, presents, or uses any record, document, or thing knowing it to be false and with purpose to mislead a public servant who is or may be engaged in such criminal investigation or official proceeding.

Tampering with physical evidence is a felony and punishable by up to five years in prison.

Section 1320 Nita Employment Code—Diversion of Employment Benefits

(1) Any person who is entrusted with money that is intended to be used in obtaining employment benefits and willfully fails to apply such money for such purpose and wrongfully diverts the funds to a use other than that for which the funds were received shall be guilty of a public offense.

(2) If the amount diverted is more than $1,000, the person shall be guilty of a felony punishable by confinement in prison for one to three years, or by a fine of up to $10,000, or by confinement in the county jail for up to one year.

(3) If the amount diverted is $1,000 or less, the person shall be guilty of a misdemeanor punishable by confinement in the county jail for up to six months, or by a fine of up to $1,000, or both.

IN THE DISTRICT COURT
OF THE STATE OF NITA
COUNTY OF DARROW

Verdict Form

THE STATE OF NITA	)	
	)	Case No. CR-2201-23
vs.	)	JURY VERDICT
	)	
SARAH HANNA BAKER,	)	
Defendant.	)	
	)	

We, the jury, return the following verdict, and each of us concurs in this verdict:

[Choose the appropriate verdict]

I. NOT GUILTY

We, the Jury, find the Defendant, Sarah H. Baker, **NOT GUILTY**.

Presiding Juror ______________________.

II. GUILTY

We, the Jury, find the Defendant, Sarah H. Baker, **GUILTY** of the crime of:

____ Murder in the First Degree

____ Murder in the Second Degree

____ Voluntary Manslaughter

Presiding Juror _________________________.